AF473786

THE WAR AGAINST

JAPAN

1941–1945

Published by IWM, Lambeth Road, London SE1 6HZ
iwm.org.uk

ISBN 978-1-911748-01-4

A catalogue record for this book is available from the British Library.
Printed and bound by Printer Trento
Colour reproduction by DL Imaging
Index by Susie Marques
Book design by Tamsin Tillier Ogilvie

Front cover: IWM (NYF 41740 / artistic rendition 2026)
Back cover: IWM (SE 2138 / artistic rendition 2026)

THE WAR AGAINST JAPAN 1941–1945

Stephen Walton

CONTENTS

INTRODUCTION

44
44

The Second World War in South-East Asia and the Pacific played out across a vast portion of the Earth's surface. It encompassed immense land masses such as China, India and Burma alongside the smallest islands and atolls and all the ocean in-between. It was a uniquely complex and challenging conflict, both for those who planned and fought it at the time, and for those who have studied it since. Its geopolitical consequences after 1945 were just as profound and long-lasting as those of the war against Nazi Germany and fascist Italy. Yet for many of the Allied military personnel who took part in it, and for many later commentators, the war against Japan was seen as having been greatly overshadowed by the war against the European dictators. This was in part a reflection of the wartime 'Germany First' policy agreed between Britain and the USA to prioritise the defeat of Nazi Germany over that of Imperial Japan – a policy with which many, particularly in America, disagreed. Many other factors have contributed to this perception of the 'forgotten war', about which there is still considerably less historical literature than that regarding the war in the West.

This book is based primarily around the rich collections of the Imperial War Museums (IWM). Large numbers of British and Commonwealth service personnel and civilians found themselves in many of the geographical areas affected by the conflict, in others they were present only in relatively small numbers or not at all. IWM's coverage of the whole Asia-Pacific war is therefore not comprehensive, but where possible I have included extracts from oral and written personal testimony to highlight the individual experiences of some of those who were there. The book also contains numerous images from the IWM's photograph collections alongside artefacts, documents, works of art and printed sources. These can provide only a very limited insight into what IWM has to offer, and it is hoped that readers will be encouraged to discover more for themselves.

Some consideration is due regarding place names and vocabulary, both of which can present difficulty and confusion. Among many examples of the former are the names of locations and camps where prisoners of war (POWs) in Thailand were held, many of which have historically been given multiple different spellings. During the war the country itself was, and

PREVIOUS PAGE Abandoned amphibious vehicles on the seafront at Betio, Tarawa Atoll, November 1943. The Japanese had made a stronghold of Tarawa in the Gilbert Islands, inflicting heavy casualties on US forces at the start of their long campaign to retake the Pacific islands.

A British government poster produced after the 1943 Cairo Conference, quoting an extract from the joint US, British and Chinese Declaration. An inset shows the relative size of the UK compared with the Asia–Pacific theatre of war.

"... the three Allies, in harmony with those of the United Nations at war with Japan, will continue to persevere in the serious and prolonged operations necessary to procure the unconditional surrender of Japan."

From the general statement issued at Cairo on December 1st, 1943, by

Franklin D. Roosevelt · Chiang Kai-shek · Winston S. Churchill

UNION OF SOVIET SOCIALIST REPUBLICS
REPUBLIC OF CHINA
Chungking
Vladivostok
JAPANESE EMPIRE
Tokyo
SAN FRANCISCO TO TOKYO 5,292 miles
HAWAII TO TOKYO 3,960 miles
NORTH PACIFIC OCEAN
ALEUTIAN IS. (U.S.)
Delhi
INDIA
Calcutta
Bombay
BURMA
Mandalay
Rangoon
SIAM
FRENCH INDO CHINA
Hong Kong
FORMOSA (Jap.)
MANILA TO TOKYO 2,080 miles
SOUTH CHINA SEA
Manila
PHILIPPINE IS. (U.S.A.)
CALCUTTA TO SINGAPORE 1,902 miles
SINGAPORE TO HONG KONG 1,680 miles
MADANG TO TOKYO 3,045 miles
WAKE IS. (U.S.)
GUAM IS. (U.S.)
MARSHALL IS. (Jap.)
CAROLINE IS. (Jap.)
GILBERT IS. (Br.)
GT. BRITAIN TO DARWIN 11,643 miles
EQUATOR
MALAYA
SUMATRA
Singapore
BORNEO
CELEBES
NEW GUINEA
SOLOMON IS.
NETHERLANDS EAST INDIES
JAVA
Darwin
INDIAN OCEAN
CORAL SEA
FIJI IS.
COMMONWEALTH OF AUSTRALIA
SYDNEY TO SAN FRANCISCO 7,545 miles
Adelaide
Sydney
Canberra
TASMANIA
DOMINION OF NEW ZEALAND
Wellington

This shows the comparative size of Gt. Britain, in relation to the Pacific area

TERRITORY OF NEUTRAL STATES

All distances in Statute miles

GPD 365/11/4

PRINTED FOR H.M. STATIONERY OFFICE BY E. & CO. LTD. 51-345

V-J. DAY THAI-LAND 1945 John Mennie

READING THE SURRENDER PRACHI. P.O.W. CAMP.
FLAGS HIDDEN FOR YEARS APPEARED

sometimes still is, variously referred to as either Thailand or Siam, although the name was officially changed from Siam to Thailand in June 1939. The POW-built Japanese railway linking Thailand and Burma during 1943–1945 is still widely, but erroneously, known as the Burma-Siam Railway, not the Burma-Thailand, or Burma-Thai, or Thai-Burma, Railway.

Since 1989 the country previously known as Burma has been called Myanmar, and many other countries in the region have also had name changes at various times after the end of the Second World War. The common designation 'Far East' as a kind of shorthand for a large part of the region is increasingly seen as problematic, emphasising a Western or Eurocentric world view. Allied service personnel in Japanese captivity were, and largely still are, called 'Far East prisoners of war' – abbreviated to FEPOWs – and it is perhaps difficult to see how this might be changed with any facility. I have tried to be sensitive to these potential stumbling blocks without being too heavy-handed, bearing in mind that for increasing numbers of readers now and in the future many of the 'old' names and phrases will no longer be as familiar as they are to my generation.

Much personal testimony of the time, and indeed since, refers to the Japanese in derogatory and racist terms as 'Japs' or 'Nips', where these terms occur in the extracts I have used in this book, I have left them as they are. I hope this respects the integrity of the original written and spoken narratives, without condoning the use of these designations.

VJ Day, Thailand 1945. Reading the Surrender, Praychi [Pratchai] *POW Camp. Flags Hidden for Years Appeared* by John Mennie.

CHAPTER ONE

THE ROAD TO PEARL HARBOR

U.S.
U.S.

Japan made its spectacular entry into the Second World War on 7 December 1941 with the surprise attack on the US Pacific Fleet at its base in Hawaii. While it came as a seismic shock to America and the West, for Japan and its armed forces Pearl Harbor was almost a welcome relief from more than four long years of an increasingly frustrating war in the vastness of China. This conflict, which had broken out in July 1937, was usually referred to by the Japanese as the 'China Incident', otherwise known to history as the Second Sino-Japanese War. It continued right through to Japan's final defeat in 1945, although after December 1941 it became part of the 'Greater East Asia War'. This wider conflict was the culmination of decades of Japan's imperial ambition in the region, driven by the Japanese equivalent of Manifest Destiny on the one hand and ruthless exploitation of resources and people on the other.

Japanese ideas of leadership and expansion in Asia had traditionally been focused on two of its nearest neighbours, Korea and China. The ancient kingdom of Korea had become a Japanese protectorate in 1905 following the Russo-Japanese War, and in 1910 was made a colonial possession. A programme of industrialisation was accompanied by a systematic attempt to eradicate Korean culture and language.

After Japan's entry into the Second World War the colony's economy and population were exploited for the war effort, effectively turning Korea into a vast slave labour camp for Japan's benefit. This policy inevitably created unrest and resistance within the country, and as the war progressed Japan found itself having to station large numbers of troops in Korea to keep order, troops it could ill afford to spare from its fighting forces elsewhere.

Beyond Korea, Japan's 'civilizing mission' had much larger horizons, above all with regard to China. After the so-called Mukden Incident in 1931, Japanese troops marched into and occupied the Chinese state of Manchuria. It became a puppet state and was renamed Manchukuo, nominally ruled by the Chinese Emperor Puyi but in effect a military fiefdom of the powerful Japanese Kwantung Army, with little reference to the government in Tokyo. Having acquired a sizeable chunk of Chinese territory the Kwantung Army had a taste for more. It helped engineer the Marco Polo Bridge Incident in 1937,

PREVIOUS PAGE Winston Churchill and Franklin D Roosevelt, arm in arm with his son Elliott, on board HMS *Prince of Wales* at the Placentia Bay Conference, Newfoundland, August 1941. Paralysed from the waist down by polio since his late 30s, Roosevelt could not walk or stand unaided.

Traditional Chinese dadao sword. Its use by soldiers of the Chinese Twenty-Ninth Army during the 1937 Marco Polo Bridge Incident inspired the patriotic 'Sword March' ('Our swords raised over the devils' heads, hack them off!').

Chinese Nationalist (Kuomintang, KMT) flag. KMT leader Chiang Kai-shek was President of the Republic of China and Commander in Chief of the Nationalist Chinese armed forces from 1928, and a major ally of Britain and the USA in the war against Japan.

a minor skirmish between Chinese and Japanese troops at Wanping, near Peking (Beijing), which triggered the Second Sino-Japanese War. The Kwantung Army leadership, together with military hawks and imperial ideologues in Tokyo, now looked to expand Japanese control into other parts of China. Japanese forces advanced southwards from Manchukuo, towards the major cities of Shanghai and Nanking (Nanjing) – seat of the Nationalist government of Chiang Kai-shek. Shanghai fell in November 1937 after a protracted and bloody battle, while Nanking was captured the following month. Japanese soldiers there engaged in a frenzy of looting, rape and murder which by most estimates claimed the lives of at least 20,000 Chinese men, women and children.

Japan was asserting itself elsewhere too. In 1936 it signed the Anti-Comintern Pact with Nazi Germany, a militarily benign, but diplomatically significant, agreement directed against the Soviet Union. On the Japanese side it was largely prompted by perceived potential threats to their interests in China by certain aspects of Soviet foreign policy, particularly in Outer Mongolia. Soviet and Japanese forces exchanged hostilities in 1939, notably during the Battles of Khalkhin Gol, but in this instance Soviet military strength and prowess cut Japanese ambitions short. Japan's ongoing war in China also created a direct threat to France's colonial territories in South-East Asia. As with Korea, Japan viewed French Indochina (comprising what are now Vietnam, Laos and Cambodia) as ripe for economic exploitation and cultural assimilation. By the time of Pearl Harbor, its armed forces controlled much of the colony – a process greatly facilitated by France's defeat and subjugation by Adolf Hitler's forces in June 1940. The same was true for Dutch interests in the region. The Dutch East Indies (now Indonesia) were rich in natural resources and played a key role in Japan's plans, particularly after the mother country also fell to Hitler in May 1940.

Territorial expansion, military aggression and economic asset grabs were officially packaged as something else by Tokyo for public consumption at home and in the countries immediately impacted. The concept of the Greater East Asia Co-Prosperity Sphere, the ideological underpinning of all this activity, was designed to cast Japan in the light of a

Chinese soldiers man a barricade in a factory during the Shanghai, or January 28, Incident in 1932. This was a major confrontation between Chinese and Japanese armed forces in one of China's most important cities, prefiguring the Second Sino-Japanese War of 1937–1945

friendly bearer of economic progress and regional harmony. Its professed aim was to throw off the yoke of the white man's imperialist domination, replacing it with an 'Asia for the Asians' under Japanese tutelage. For many of those thus 'liberated' the brutal realities of Japan's own imperial project soon exposed this propaganda for what it was. For others, however, it was heady wine and a spur to the creation of new post-colonial identities.

By 1941 it was clear that Japan's sights were set on establishing itself as the dominant power in South-East Asia, replacing Western colonial structures and geopolitical influence with a Japanese-led 'New Order'. This was of particular concern to the two Western powers whose interests

Japanese Marines advancing into Manchuria following the 1931 Mukden Incident. A Chinese state historically contested by Japan and Russia, it was under Japanese occupation and known as Manchukuo from 1931 until 1945.

Japanese soldiers occupy the city of Kaifeng in June 1938, during the Second Sino-Japanese War. Rapid Japanese advances in that part of China had already forced Chiang Kai-shek to relocate his government from Nanking (Nanjing) to Chungking (Chongqing) further west.

in the region were most immediately threatened: Britain and the USA. The Philippines had effectively been a colonial possession of the United States since 1899 but were undergoing a protracted transition to sovereign self-government. Its armed forces remained firmly in American hands for the time being, coming under the control of the commander of the US Army Forces in the Far East, General Douglas MacArthur. For Japan, the Philippines lay directly in the path of any southward move towards the oilfields and other natural riches of the Dutch

East Indies and had to be neutralised. A continued American presence on the islands would also pose a threat to Japan's plans to seize control of the British colonial prizes of Malaya (now Malaysia), Burma (now Myanmar) and, the ultimate 'jewel in the crown', India. In these countries too Japan hoped to exploit their resources of oil, coal, rubber, tin and gold to boost the domestic economy and secure the foundations of its expanding empire.

While preoccupied with the consequences of Hitler's territorial ambitions in Europe, Britain and the USA were by no means unconcerned by Japan's aggression in China and elsewhere. American President Franklin D Roosevelt had spoken out against Japanese actions in China and in July 1941, as a result of Japanese encroachments in French Indochina, he authorised a freeze of Japanese assets in the USA and, crucially, an embargo on petroleum and other vital exports to Japan.

These developments accelerated Japanese preparations for war, although attempts were made on both sides to avoid this outcome in the immediate term through diplomacy. Official and unofficial peace envoys shuttled between Washington and Tokyo in the autumn of 1941 with the blessings of both President Roosevelt and Emperor Hirohito, but prospects of a peaceful settlement were rapidly fading. The warmongers in Tokyo were heartened by the appointment in October 1941 of the hawkish Army Minister General Hideki Tōjō as prime minister. In the following month, Tōjō rejected American demands for a withdrawal from China as a precondition for the resumption of trading relations, and the course was set for war.

British Prime Minister Winston Churchill was also mindful of the growing Japanese threat to his country's interests further east. One of Churchill's main political objectives was to bring the hitherto neutral and isolationist USA into the war, not just as the 'arsenal of democracy' through the Lend-Lease Act but as a fully-fledged belligerent. A major step along this path was the August 1941 conference between Churchill and Roosevelt and their advisers at Placentia Bay in Newfoundland. Its main outcome was the Atlantic Charter, setting out joint democratic principles and broad war aims, but the two leaders also drafted an official warning to Japan to cease its aggressive stance or face consequences. Unfortunately, the note that

Emperor Hirohito of Japan, photographed in 1935. The country's longest-reigning monarch to date (1926–1989). Hirohito's role in Japan's wars of aggression is still the subject of debate and controversy.

Eleventh hour diplomacy: Japanese Ambassador to the USA Admiral Kichisaburō Nomura (left) and Special Envoy Saburō Kurusu (with hat) leaving the White House two weeks before Pearl Harbor. As Ambassador in Berlin, Kurusu had signed the 1940 Tripartite Pact with Nazi Germany and fascist Italy.

was finally sent to Tokyo was so watered down on American insistence that it was practically meaningless, and only served to further encourage the Japanese war party. The latter had already taken comfort from Hitler's invasion of the USSR in June 1941, which promised to distract Joseph Stalin from any entanglement with Japan on his eastern frontiers.

From mid-October 1941 onwards, with no signs that Japan was taking any practical steps towards a resolution of the situation, preparations for war accelerated in the USA as well as in Japan. Diplomatic contacts continued but now looked more like polite window-dressing. The US ambassador in Tokyo, Joseph Grew, warned that Japan could launch hostilities at any time, including a possible attack on Pearl Harbor. Grew's prediction was not long in becoming reality. On 26 November, Admiral Chūichi Nagumo's carrier-based 1st Air Fleet 'Mobile Force' (*Kidō Butai*) left its anchorage in the Kurile (Kuril) Islands and embarked on the long, hazardous voyage to Hawaii. Its mission was to destroy the fighting capability of the US Pacific Fleet, assuring Japanese superiority in the crucial first stages of a war that now seemed certain and imminent. The last diplomatic civilities between Washington and Tokyo were still being observed as Nagumo's Mobile Force arrived at its destination, and as the first Japanese bombs rained down on Hawaii on Sunday 7 December 1941. Japan's war against the West had begun.

CHAPTER TWO

'A DATE WHICH WILL LIVE IN INFAMY'

The early Sunday morning peace of the US Pacific Fleet base on O'ahu Island was shattered at 7.50am local time, when the first wave of Japanese fighters, dive-bombers, torpedo-bombers and other aircraft burst out of the sky. By the time the last attacker left two hours later, carnage prevailed. Around 20 ships had been sunk or badly damaged, notably the battleships USS *Arizona*, *Oklahoma*, *California* and *West Virginia*. All four were sunk; however, with the exception of the *Arizona*, each was later salvaged and returned to service. In addition to the warships and other vessels at anchor, the Japanese also wreaked havoc on Hawaii's airfields at Wheeler, Hickam, Kāne'ohe and Ewa, destroying or damaging almost 300 aircraft. The human cost was equally stark, with 2,403 American service personnel and civilians dead and 1,178 wounded. Around half of the fatalities were due to the catastrophic detonation of USS *Arizona*'s forward ammunition magazine, which sealed her fate.

On the face of it, Admiral Nagumo's forces had dealt a mortal blow to American naval power in the Pacific. However, several factors ensured that it had a fighting chance of recovery. Nagumo was subsequently criticised for not finishing the job and knocking out the base's repair facilities and fuel storage installations, which would have crippled Pearl Harbor completely. He was fearful of an American counterattack and wanted to withdraw his forces at the earliest opportunity. Crucially, the US Pacific Fleet's aircraft carriers escaped the inferno, both USS *Lexington* and *Enterprise* being away from O'ahu at the time. This gave the Americans a vital advantage in the carrier-based naval war to come.

None of this detracted from the immediate impact of Pearl Harbor. It seemed that the American giant had been caught napping, and the country had suffered a national humiliation of epic proportions. The following day President Roosevelt addressed a joint session of Congress in solemn tones, reading, appropriately, from a black notebook:

> Yesterday, December 7 1941 – a date which will live in infamy – the United States of America was suddenly and deliberately attacked by naval and air forces of the Empire

PREVIOUS PAGE The opening moments of Operation 'Z', photographed by a Japanese aviator. A torpedo bomber can be seen banking away to the right of the column of water thrown up by a hit on USS *West Virginia*, anchored in Battleship Row.

A rescue launch approaches the blazing and sinking USS *West Virginia*, hit by 7 torpedoes and 2 bombs which killed 106 of her crew. The ship was subsequently raised, repaired and able to participate in later naval actions at Leyte, Iwo Jima and Okinawa.

> of Japan... I ask that the Congress declare that since the unprovoked and dastardly attack by Japan... a state of war has existed between the United States and the Japanese Empire.

Admiral Isoroku Yamamoto, Commander in Chief of the Japanese Combined Fleet, who masterminded the Pearl Harbor attack.

Roosevelt signing the US declaration of war against Japan on 8 December 1941. Churchill had already notified Tokyo that Britain was at war with Japan following the landings in Malaya and air raids on Singapore and Hong Kong.

The following evening, in one of his regular 'Fireside Chat' radio broadcasts, Roosevelt spoke directly to the American people:

> The sudden criminal attacks perpetrated by the Japanese in the Pacific provide the climax of a decade of international immorality. Powerful and resourceful gangsters have banded together to make war upon the whole human race. Their challenge has now been flung at the United States of America. The Japanese have treacherously violated the long-standing peace between us. Many American soldiers and sailors have been killed by enemy action. American ships have been sunk. American airplanes have been destroyed. The Congress and the people of the United States have accepted that challenge. Together with other free peoples, we are now fighting to maintain our right to live among our world neighbours in freedom and in common decency, without fear of assault...We are now in this war. We are all in it, all the way. Every single man, woman and child is a partner in the most tremendous undertaking of our American history.

As newspaper and radio reports of the events in Hawaii reached into homes and workplaces across the United States, Americans tried to come to terms with a suddenly changed world. As Burton Stein, a teenager in Chicago at that time, later recalled:

> Pearl Harbor was profoundly shocking. I think Americans had gotten accustomed to the possibility that thcy would really not be in the war, that they were doing what they could to resist Hitler... I remember that day of 7 December... the interruption of the Sunday football game... We were very surprised that this could have happened, the Japanese seemed a very long way away from anything, at that time I certainly had no awareness of what was going on in South-East Asia.

The attack on Pearl Harbor propelled the United States out of its isolationist complacency and, ultimately, ensured the defeat of the Axis powers. In many crucial respects it rallied the country around its president and welded the nation together in unity of purpose. But it also left deep scars in the national psyche. Bewilderment and anger that such a thing could have happened persisted. There were six official wartime investigations into the reasons for the disaster, and a major Congressional enquiry after the war. These found no fault with Roosevelt or those in high government office, although entirely unsubstantiated theories circulated then and since that the president knew about the planned attack and allowed it to happen in order to force his country into a war it didn't want to engage with. The most prominent career casualty was that of the Commander in Chief of the Pacific Fleet, Admiral Husband Kimmel, who was accused of dereliction of duty, relieved of his command and retired. The post-war Congressional enquiry somewhat modified this verdict, attributing to him errors of judgement rather than negligence. The senior army commander in Hawaii, Lieutenant General Walter Short, whose responsibilities included air defence, was also relieved of his duties.

In the search for scapegoats, other American citizens were also excluded from the 'united nation'. Large numbers of Japanese-Americans who had been left alone by the authorities in their communities now came under intense official and popular suspicion. Eventually, over 100,000 of them – mainly resident on the West Coast, nearest to Japan – were evicted from their homes and interned in special camps. A similar process occurred over the border in Canada, a British Dominion, where it was likewise considered that Japanese-Canadians living on the western seaboard were potential 'fifth columnists' and could not be trusted not to indulge in pro-Japanese agitation and subversion.

As shocking as it was, the strike on Pearl Harbor was just the curtain-raiser for a *Blitzkrieg*-style assault by Japan's armed forces on a broad front in the region. On the same day as destruction was inflicted on the Pacific Fleet in Hawaii, America's major Pacific bases on Guam, Wake and Midway

Remember December 7th! US Office of War Information poster from 1942, exhorting Americans to rally around the national war effort. The words at the top of the poster are from Abraham Lincoln's 1863 Gettysburg Address.

…we here highly resolve that these dead shall not have died in vain…
REMEMBER DEC. 7th!

were also attacked. Japanese shells had already hit the north-east coast of Malaya ahead of a full-scale invasion of the British colony, and Japanese bombers appeared over Singapore. In the next 24 hours they also targeted Luzon and Mindanao in the Philippines, while Japanese troops headed for Hong Kong, Shanghai and Tientsin (Tianjin) in China. Everywhere, it seemed, the forces of Imperial Japan were on the attack.

The 'chief executive' of this dizzying multi-pronged campaign of conquest was the Commander in Chief of the Japanese Combined Fleet, Admiral Isoroku Yamamoto. An urbane and highly intelligent commander who had spent time in the USA both as a student and later as naval attaché in Washington, Yamamoto was the Imperial Japanese Navy's leading expert and advocate of naval air power. It was perhaps ironic that the architect of Operation 'Z' against Pearl Harbor

A fireball rises above Kāne'ohe Naval Air Station, Hawaii. Most of the sea planes based there were destroyed ahead of the main strike on the Pacific Fleet ships, to prevent their use against the Japanese.

Imperial Japanese Navy submarine I-26. She claimed the first US Merchant Marine casualty of the Pacific war with the sinking of SS *Cynthia Olson* on 7 December 1941, immediately after the attack on Pearl Harbor. All trace of the ship's crew was subsequently lost.

had for many years also been strongly opposed to the war party in Tokyo and advised against risking hostilities with the Western powers.

He had reportedly told Prime Minister Konoe, in relation to his assessment of Japan's chances in such a war, that 'we can run wild for six months or a year, but after that I have utterly no confidence. I hope you will try to avoid war with America'. As precisely that war became an increasing probability, Yamamoto and his staff devised the Pearl Harbor operation with the immediate objective of destroying the US Pacific Fleet in a pre-emptive strike, thus maximising Japan's chances of then being able to achieve its strategic goals in the Asia-Pacific area.

For the relatively short period in which Japan seemed to be victorious on all fronts, Yamamoto was the hero of the hour in his country and his prestige among other military and political leaders skyrocketed accordingly. In his 'Fireside Chat' quoted earlier, even Roosevelt had paid grudging respect and acknowledged that 'our enemies have performed a brilliant feat of deception, perfectly timed and executed with great skill'. Not just the United States but the Western powers as a whole had once again been wrong-footed and humiliated by swift and ruthless aggression, just as they had been in Europe in the dark days of 1939 and 1940.

Memorial Certificate for Private Jack Feldman of the US Army Air Forces, killed at Hickam Field during the Pearl Harbor attack. There were 432 casualties that day on Hawaii's main army airfield and bomber base.

IN GRATEFUL MEMORY OF

Private Jack H. Feldman, A.S.No. 13027061,

WHO DIED IN THE SERVICE OF HIS COUNTRY AT

Hickam Field, Territory of Hawaii, December 7, 1941.

HE STANDS IN THE UNBROKEN LINE OF PATRIOTS WHO HAVE DARED TO DIE

THAT FREEDOM MIGHT LIVE, AND GROW, AND INCREASE ITS BLESSINGS.

FREEDOM LIVES, AND THROUGH IT, HE LIVES—

IN A WAY THAT HUMBLES THE UNDERTAKINGS OF MOST MEN

Franklin D Roosevelt

PRESIDENT OF THE UNITED STATES OF AMERICA

CHAPTER THREE

THE FALL OF MALAYA AND SINGAPORE

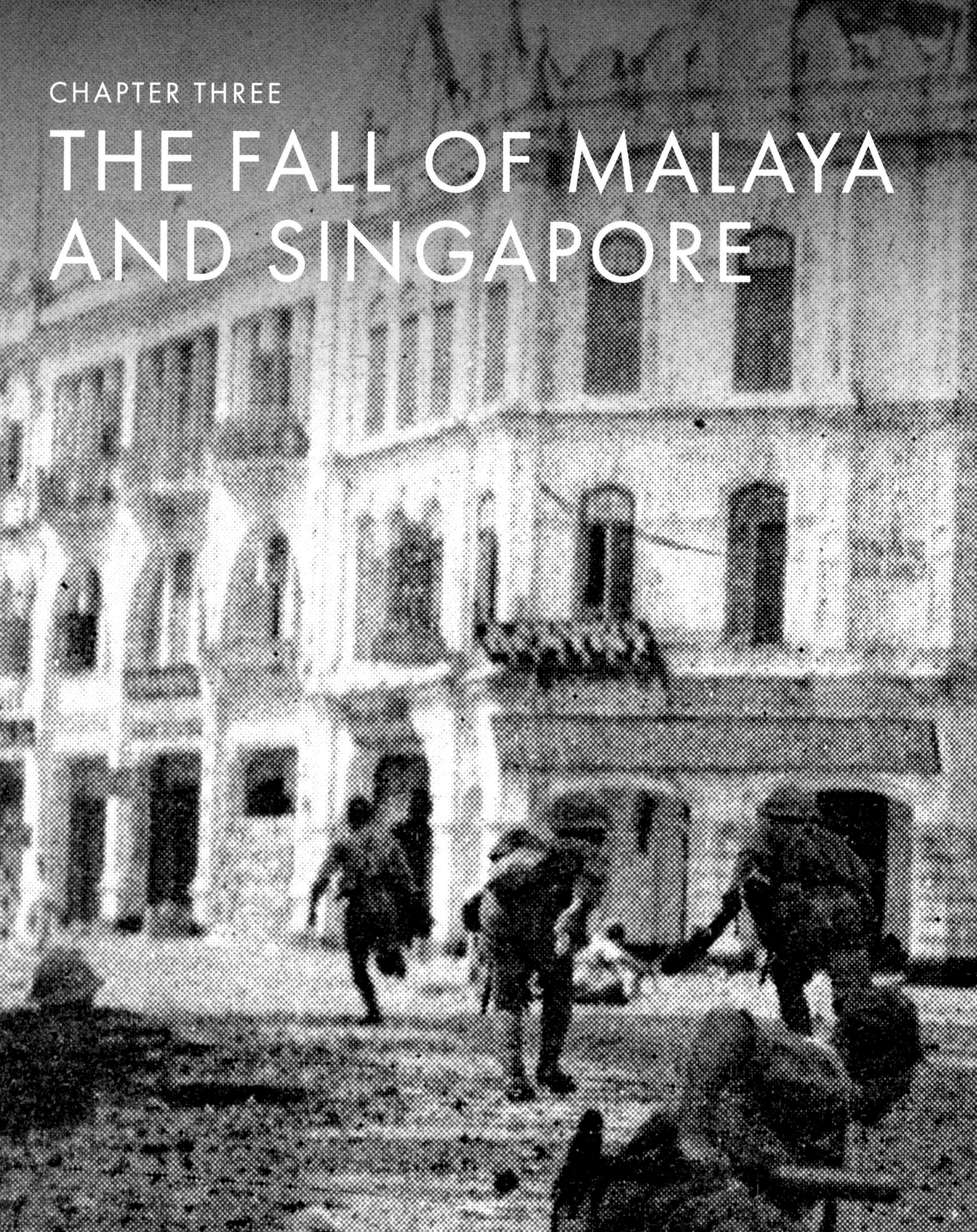

ith the apparent success of the Pearl Harbor operation, Japan's campaign of conquest in South-East Asia and the Pacific could commence. The overall direction of this formidable undertaking was in the hands of Field Marshal Count Hisaichi Terauchi, commander of the Southern Expeditionary Army Group. Headquartered in Saigon (Japanese-occupied French Indochina) for the first phase of the campaign, it comprised four Armies and two Air Divisions whose primary objectives were the Philippines, Hong Kong, Malaya and Singapore, and the Dutch East Indies. Once these had been secured, further potential prizes lay beyond.

Tasked with the invasion of the Malayan peninsula and the island of Singapore at its southern tip was General Tomoyuki Yamashita's Twenty-Fifth Army. Yamashita had a tendency to fall out with his political and military masters, including Emperor Hirohito and Prime Minister Tōjō, and had spent much of his time in relatively unimportant posts abroad. At the time of his appointment to command in Malaya, he was kicking his heels as commander of the Kwantung Army in Manchuria – although this was perhaps a good enough springboard from which to propel himself to popular acclaim as the 'Tiger of Malaya'.

Rich in natural resources, primarily rubber and tin, Malaya had increasingly come under British control from the late 18th century onwards. At the time of the Japanese invasion, British Malaya was a complex and delicately balanced political and territorial patchwork, comprising the Federated and Unfederated Malay States and the Straits Settlements, including Singapore, with a mix of direct and indirect colonial administration alongside the continued role of the traditional Malay rulers in each state. The strategic importance of Singapore was emphasised with the construction of a major naval base after the First World War. This made the 'island fortress' the epicentre of Britain's defence of her colonial possessions in the wider region, commanding vital sea routes between the Indian Ocean and the Pacific. What made Malaya economically and Singapore strategically important to Britain was precisely what also made them prime targets for Japan. It was Yamashita's time to shine.

In terms of chronology, Japan's war with the West started in

PREVIOUS PAGE Japanese troops on the streets of Kuala Lumpur, Malaya, January 1942. Pre-war development of the rubber industry led to boomtown conditions, but under Japanese occupation thousands of the city's Chinese and Indian inhabitants were killed or deported as forced labour.

British Royal Engineers place demolition charges in a bridge during the retreat in Malaya, as civilian traffic continues. According to the original caption, Chinese rickshaws are 'loaded with rice from abandoned government stocks'.

Malaya, not at Pearl Harbor. Shortly after 1am on 7 December 1941, the Japanese invasion force approaching the north-east coast of Malaya at Kota Bharu began shelling shore defences, two hours before Japanese aircraft struck Hawaii. In the grand scheme of things it hardly mattered, as both the USA and Britain were woefully unprepared for what hit them on that day. British defences in Malaya were thinly spread and undermanned, in part due to historic conflicts between military planners and the civil administration. The situation in Singapore was little better, despite its much-vaunted strategic importance. From September 1939 onwards, the war in Europe had in any case taken precedence over military preparedness in South-East Asia, and both Malaya and Singapore ranked low in the allocation of resources. The naval base on Singapore Island had for most of its existence been without warships of any description, and it was only in October 1941 that the British Admiralty reluctantly ordered for the battlecruiser HMS *Repulse* and battleship HMS *Prince of Wales*, and the aircraft carrier HMS *Indomitable*, to be sent to Singapore. Unfortunately, the *Indomitable* failed to live up to her name on this occasion and ran aground in the West Indies on her maiden voyage, leaving the other two ships to form the main naval deterrent.

The Japanese plan of attack on Malaya provided for landings in force not only at Kota Bharu but also at Singora and Patani, across the border on Thailand's Kra Isthmus, from where the Japanese would advance overland into northern Malaya and capture objectives on the west coast. This element of the plan was facilitated by the fact that the Thai government was effectively a pro-Japanese military dictatorship led by Plaek Phibunsongkhram – better known in the West as Pibul Songgram. There was some initial resistance on the part of the local Thai Army units, but it was ordered to cease on 9 December and Plaek signed a formal military alliance with Japan later that month.

Facing the main Japanese force at Kota Bharu was the 8th Indian Infantry Brigade, which was unable to prevent the invaders from establishing a beachhead despite putting up fierce resistance. Supportive airpower was lacking after the Royal Air Force (RAF) evacuated the local airfield as a result of erroneous reports that the Japanese had broken through. Muhammad Ismail Khan, a 2/10th Baluch Regiment officer attached to 8th Indian Brigade headquarters, was there when the invasion began. He had been tasked with finding out what was happening on the landing beaches, and on his way back to Brigade HQ took what must have been one of the first Japanese POWs in Malaya:

> As I crossed this little plank bridge I found a [Japanese] soldier standing in front of me without his little rubber boots... without his putties, the trousers were hanging on his feet. And he had lost his steel helmet but his rifle was there in his hand and around his belt there were a few pouches of ammunition and a few grenades. So I looked at him and without hesitation I walked towards him... He saw me, he dropped his rifle and put his hands up... I made him sit pillion [on Khan's motorbike] and I drove him up to the Brigade headquarters. On the way some incredulous eyes were watching me, Indian soldiers, some British officers, and I was waving at them with one hand:'Jap! Jap! Jap!' and I was going along laughing away like hell...When I entered the Brigade headquarters... I met Richard Dent, our Brigade Major... He said 'My God, where the hell did you get him?' I said, 'I met him on the way back from the beach.'

Further west, the 11th Indian Division was positioned around Jitra, facing the Japanese forces advancing from Thailand. A daring British plan to advance into southern Thailand to deny Singora and Patani to the Japanese landing forces, codenamed 'Matador', had been abandoned at the last minute on the advice of the General Officer Commanding Malaya, Lieutenant General Arthur Percival. Poor training and poor command decisions combined to cause significant casualties and confusion among the troops of 11th Indian Division, which soon withdrew to Alor Star (Alor Setar). This was the start of what became a fighting retreat down the length of the Malay peninsula, characterised by desperate and improvised local defences against overwhelming Japanese superiority in the air and on the ground. Demoralised British and Indian troops stood little real chance against mostly battle-

hardened Japanese soldiers, veterans of their country's long war in China. The Japanese had tanks, while the defenders did not, and were expert at moving swiftly across country and outflanking defensive positions. They also enjoyed almost unchallenged air superiority as RAF airfields and aircraft were systematically attacked and destroyed from bases in southern Thailand and French Indochina.

As the defensive dominos started falling in Malaya, another disaster was unfolding offshore. Having arrived at Singapore, HMS *Prince of Wales* and *Repulse* in company with four destroyers were ordered to put to sea on 8 December in a last-minute and ultimately futile attempt to disrupt the Japanese landings at Kota Bharu and points north. The naval expedition was designated Force Z and was commanded by Admiral Sir Tom Phillips, who told his men: 'We are out looking for trouble and no doubt we shall find it.' It didn't happen quite as Phillips was expecting or hoping; the force was discovered by Japanese reconnaissance planes and a submarine, and the Admiral reluctantly ordered his ships to break off the expedition and return to Singapore. They got as far as the waters off Kuantan – where Japanese forces were, quite erroneously, also reported to be landing – and in the late morning of 10 December Japanese bombers found them and launched a devastating aerial attack. Both *Repulse* and *Prince of Wales* were sent to the bottom of the ocean, the latter ship taking 'Tom Thumb' Phillips with it. 840 sailors were lost, but the death toll would have been far higher without the tenacious rescue efforts of the Force Z destroyers. Although much smaller in scale, the impact of this event on the British public and politicians was in many ways comparable to that of Pearl Harbor in the USA. A dark time had become that much darker, and the road ahead that much more difficult to discern.

It was not just British and Commonwealth military forces that were being pushed ever southwards by the Japanese advance. Civilians too, particularly the country's European residents, were on the move in large numbers. Many of these were evacuated from the island of Penang when it was abandoned to the Japanese in the middle of December, joining a steady stream of refugees heading south to Johore and, if the worst happened, to the supposed safe haven of Singapore

PREVIOUS PAGE Dead Japanese soldiers next to their Type 95 Ha-Go light tank, knocked out by the Australians at Muar in January 1942. The British had judged Malaya to be largely unsuitable terrain for the deployment of tanks, but Japan used the Ha-Go successfully there and in other campaigns during the early stages of the war.

Brewster Buffalos of 243 Squadron RAF over the Malayan jungle. The mainstay of the fighter defence of Malaya and Singapore, the American-built Buffalo was notoriously prone to technical problems and was generally no match for its Japanese opponents.

Island. Allan Gerard, Malaya's Chief Electrical Engineer responsible for the country's power supply, witnessed the effects of the fighting in the city of Kuala Lumpur, capital of the Federated Malay States. He wrote in his diary on 3 January 1942:

> Nipponese forces still advancing. It seems obvious now that only a miracle can save KL [Kuala Lumpur]. The town is emptying rapidly, and what with the bomb damaged and scarred buildings, grass growing quite unrestrictedly, bomb craters in the road, smashed or burnt-out cars still standing on the roadside, and a general absence of human beings, it makes me feel very sick at heart to view it and recall that only a few weeks before it was a happy, busy and attractive town...[9 January 1942] The end appears to be in sight now, the enemy are this side of Rawang. Reconnaissance planes are frequently snooping over, but I believe there is no bombing. By day the skyline is marred by dense black clouds as rubber stocks are burned, at night they appear as big red glowing patches in the sky. Engineers and sappers have already cut the bridges and placed the [explosive] charges in. The contents of shops like Robinsons are being given away, the recipients queuing up for stuff in order to avoid uncontrolled looting. The police have already disappeared.

Shortly afterwards Gerard was ordered to render the main power station useless to the Japanese by wrecking its vital components, after which he joined the refugees. His diary entries encapsulate the chaos, destruction and human cost of the events he was caught up in along with millions of others in Malaya:

> The town already had a stricken look and a few scared people were trying to make a getaway in old cars and even rickshaws and bullock carts. The journey was uneventful until we reached Kajang. This pleasant little township had been attacked in force by the [Japanese] air force the previous afternoon and was bombed. When the scared inhabitants began running away the airmen machine-gunned them. Corpses were lying about all over the place

Twilight of the battleship era: HMS *Prince of Wales* crew abandoning ship after she fell victim to Japanese naval air power off the coast of Malaya on 10 December 1941. The photograph was taken from the destroyer HMS *Express* which assisted in the rescue efforts.

> and just beginning to smell. I saw one chap, a Chinese, wheeling a body away by putting it on his bicycle. In one corner of the crossroads the corpses were piled up... The road was ornamented with wrecked cars and lorries, they had either crashed into the rubble or been pushed off the road, some had been machine-gunned, some bombed, but I think most had crashed during night driving, black roads, no lights, reckless drivers making the necessary combination.

The defence of southern Malaya, more specifically the state of Johore, rested mainly with the Australian 8th Division commanded by Major General Gordon Bennett. The Australians, later strengthened by an Indian brigade, temporarily delayed the Japanese advance around Gemas and Muar, but it was not enough to save Johore. At the end of January, General Arthur Percival sought and received permission to withdraw all Allied forces across the Johore Strait to Singapore. The last Allied soldiers to cross from the mainland to the island did so on 31 January, blowing a gap in the causeway behind them. Several days before that reinforcements had arrived in Singapore, mainly comprising the British 18th Division alongside Indian and Australian forces. The island now had the equivalent of four army divisions to defend it, but for the most part those who had survived the fighting in Malaya were exhausted and demoralised, and many of the new arrivals were poorly trained and inadequately armed.

General Sir Archibald Wavell, at the head of the short-lived American-British-Dutch-Australian Command (ABDACOM) in South-East Asia, had made a whirlwind tour of the Malaya-Singapore theatre of operations in early January 1942, and sent a highly pessimistic assessment of the situation to Winston Churchill. The latter had been appalled to learn that Singapore Island was not the impregnable fortress he, and many others, had fondly imagined it to be, declaring that the city, if not the island, 'must be converted into a citadel and defended to the death. No surrender can be contemplated'. British hopes were partly buoyed by the numerical superiority of the Allied defenders, comprising some 70,000 combat troops, over the Japanese force of around 35,000 set to attack them. But the defenders were on the back foot in almost every respect and the Japanese were on a high of conquest, rendering the numbers effectively meaningless.

Yamashita's men landed on the island in force on 8 February, choosing the north-western sector which was relatively lightly defended and difficult to hold at the best of times. Percival was expecting the main thrust to come from the north-east and had arranged his defences accordingly, with little capacity to alter them at short notice. Among those facing the Japanese as they launched their assault across the Johore Strait was Lance Corporal Jack Egan, serving with the 2/30th Battalion of 8th Division, Australian Imperial Force. As he wrote later in captivity:

Australian Army nurses wait to disembark at Singapore, October 1941. As war with Japan looked increasingly likely, Australian service personnel were among those sent to the colony to prepare for a possible invasion.

> Our position was a good one, largely sheltered from observation by rubber trees, and looking across a patch of tidal swamp covered with low bushes across the smooth waters of the straits to the opposite shore, perhaps 1,500 yards away... Planes came over and bombed and machine-gunned us, indeed everyone and everything on the island, and from then on we knew no peace. We could hear tractors bringing [the Japanese] guns up at night and from intermittent the shelling became almost incessant...The shelling continued at night as well as during the daytime and was particularly active during mealtimes. Where, you will ask, was our own artillery all this time? And where the planes we were told to expect, and of which we had seen a few specimens, always (except one) when there were no enemy planes about?

Although the Australians' artillery soon began to give as good as it got, Egan considered that the initial advantage had been irretrievably lost. The first Japanese assaults were disrupted by machine-gun and small arms fire, but they kept on coming:

> Again and again they tried... I take my hat off to the Japanese soldiers who faced that open stretch of water again and again. They were the bravest of brave men and they never looked like succeeding... Imagine our astonishment and resentment at this moment to be ordered to withdraw. I cannot convey to you our amazement and disgust as we left our positions with sluggish steps and sullen tempers... I think every man of us knew in his heart, that the Malayan campaign was lost... It appears that the enemy had landed elsewhere, and with a force operating in our rear had practically cut us off.

Having landed successfully at multiple points, the Japanese advanced rapidly towards Singapore City, inflicting heavy casualties on the defenders as they went and creating a sense of impending doom in the city itself. Wavell's orders to Percival's forces became increasingly desperate as the situation deteriorated, informing them that 'our whole fighting reputation is at stake and the honour of the British Empire... Commanders and senior officers must lead their troops and if necessary die with them.'

But Wavell was in the comparative safety of Java. On the ground in Singapore soldiers and civilians got through each day as best they could. Arthur Sleep, a civil servant and Air Raid Precautions (ARP) squad leader in the city at the time of the Japanese assault, was one of many inhabitants who initially put their faith in the official pronouncements:

Indian soldiers on board the troopship *Devonshire* bound for Singapore from Bombay (Mumbai), February 1942. Among the last troops to reach Singapore before it fell to the Japanese, they are cleaning their Lee-Enfield rifles ready for action.

> The loss of Hong Kong [on 25 December 1941], the evacuation of Penang and the arrival of our Penang friends to stay with us... made us realise we were in for a grim time in Singapore, but we all hoped the tide would turn and that with reinforcements our troops would recover lost ground... We all believed, and acted on the belief, that as our military experts had said that Singapore was impregnable, our troops would be able to hold the island.

Residents of the Tiong Bahru housing estate in Singapore wait for the 'all clear' in an air raid shelter. From early January 1942, as Japanese troops got closer, the city was subjected to increasingly frequent bombing raids with heavy civilian casualties.

Those who still nursed this hope were rapidly disillusioned as the Japanese steadily advanced towards the city, which was subjected to heavy and increasingly frequent air raids. Sleep and his family experienced these at close quarters:

> Soon the bomb raids became more severe and every night we took shelter two or three times beneath the stairs. The ceilings of our rooms were made of brittle asbestos sheeting

> which shattered and fell in jagged pieces when the house was bombed. Fortunately...we were on duty in the town whilst the servants were in a covered trench in the garden. The servants' quarters and the garage were completely demolished, and the ceilings had fallen in when we returned.

Death and destruction were visited on all in the city, not just relatively privileged Europeans, and the scenes witnessed by Allan Gerard in Kuala Lumpur were repeated in Singapore. Gerard was now trapped there and was doing his best to maintain the city's electricity supply. His diary records his experiences in the days following the initial Japanese landings on the island:

> [10 February] The Japs had already got artillery over onto the island and were shelling the roads, including, I soon discovered, the one I was on, and one shell burst so near that it affected my ears and left me somewhat dazed...As the day progressed the Nippon forces brought more artillery over and the shelling of the outskirts of the city increased...
>
> The gunfire on the west coast is getting louder. It sounds as though we must be falling back...Our house was situated in a compound off Holland Road, one of the main roads leading to the fighting area...This road, particularly in the early morning, was very congested with lorries, guns, light and heavy, Bren carriers etc, and the streams of blackened and soaking troops tramping citywards for a rest. Everybody looked grim and depressed. The only planes in the sky were Nipponese, and they were harassing our people particularly on the roads...
>
> [11 February] More shelling in our neighbourhood all day. The situation is now serious and already we have seen British, Indian and Australian troops walking back to Singapore without rifles or equipment. Heavy fighting is still going on and the gunfire is ceaseless. The heavy smoke from the burning oil tanks at the naval base still continues and more of these heavy columns of smoke are appearing in the sky.

At about the same time as Gerard was witnessing the collapse of Singapore's defences, Churchill was echoing

Wavell's earlier 'fight to the death' exhortations, urging his ABDA Commander in Chief that 'the battle must be fought to the bitter end at all costs... There must at this stage be no thought of saving the troops or sparing the population.' But Churchill was far removed from the field of battle, and his senior soldiers on the spot were being forced to view things differently. On 12 February Percival ordered a last-ditch defensive perimeter to be thrown around the city, but it was a Canute-like gesture amid mounting chaos, panic, desertion and the collapse of vital infrastructure, including the island's water supplies. By 15 February, Percival and his senior commanders had run out of all feasible options other than capitulation. Contrary to Churchill's apocalyptic vision, British and Commonwealth troops were to be saved as far as was now possible, and the civil population must also be spared the horrors of desperate urban fighting.

The events leading up to the Allied surrender in Singapore were later recorded by one of those most closely involved.

One of Singapore's coastal defence guns demonstrating its firepower. The colony's defences were primarily designed to repel an invasion from the open sea rather than the Malayan mainland. Although they could be traversed inland, these guns were far more effective against ships than ground troops.

A car being tipped into Singapore harbour by British soldiers during desperate last-minute attempts to deny potential assets to the Japanese.

Major Cyril Wild was then serving on the staff of General Sir Lewis Heath's III Indian Corps:

> At about 21.00 hrs on 13 February 42 Lieutenant General Sir Lewis Heath...informed me that at a conference which he had had that day with Lieutenant General A E Percival, GOC Malaya, it had become clear that if the situation continued to deteriorate we should have to ask for terms. He added that, as Malaya Command had sent all of their Japanese-speaking officers out of the country, General Percival had asked him if he had any such officers available, and that he had given my name. He then said: 'In case the situation arises, you must therefore hold yourself in readiness to go through the lines and make the first contact with the enemy, to arrange a meeting between their commander and General Percival'...
>
> On 15 February '42 I accompanied [General Heath] to the final conference in the underground 'battle-box' at Fort Canning. Lt Gen A E Percival invited a review of the situation from the senior officers present. I recall in particular that the [Chief Engineer] Brigadier Simpson said that no more water would be available in Singapore from some time during the next day (16 Feb); [it was also said] that Bofors ammunition would be exhausted by that afternoon (15 Feb), and that another class of ammunition... was likewise exhausted. The decision to ask for terms was taken without a dissentient voice.

Some confusion remained as to the precise timing of a ceasefire to facilitate a meeting between Percival and Yamashita. Wild expressed his frustration at Percival's 'painful inability to give a decision... when points of operational importance were referred to him', but later that same day Percival, Wild and two other officers finally made their way to Yamashita's temporary headquarters at Bukit Timah:

> As we drove up the Bukit Timah road I looked with interest to see whether the fighting was still in progress, as by then it was long after 16.00 hours [the time agreed for the ceasefire]. I felt then and consider now that no-one in the two cars had the least idea whether the war was supposed to

Black smoke from burning oil tanks on Singapore Naval Base spreads over the city. Completed in 1938 at astronomical cost, the base boasted what was then the largest dry dock in the world and was among the reasons why Churchill called the island 'the Gibraltar of the East'.

> be over or not. There was some [anti-aircraft] fire at low-flying enemy aircraft and a little small-arms fire but I do not recall that there was any gunfire...Again our party had to leave the cars and walk up the road until met by the Japanese.

The two opposing commanders in Malaya quickly agreed on the cessation of hostilities and unconditional British surrender, to come into effect later that evening. Yamashita told Percival's party that he had been ordered to begin the final assault on Singapore at midnight, and according to Wild 'expressed his relief' that he was now spared this undertaking, not for any humanitarian reasons, but because his own forces were reaching their limits. The 'Tiger of Malaya' had won his laurels, including a massive haul of around 130,000 POWs. In the war-scarred city, soon to be renamed *Syonan-to* by the

Ronald Searle
Banzai!
Ban Zai! First days, Singapore 1942
16 Feb 1942

Japanese, Allan Gerard concluded his diary laconically: 'About 8pm a messenger arrived to tell us that an armistice had been arranged, and we noticed that the sound of battle had died away.' So ended what Churchill famously termed 'the worst disaster and largest capitulation in British history'. Jack Egan and his Australian comrades were profoundly affected by the experience:

> We looked back over the campaign, and knew now that every false hope was shattered, that we had never had a chance, had never been meant to win. We knew now that it had not been even a campaign, but a shimozzle, ending in a shambles. I burnt my brief diary, and some of my cobbers burnt the photos of their wives, mothers and sweethearts so that they would not be ridiculed or ill-treated by our captors.

It was another traumatic moment for Britain and her allies across the globe. For Churchill it seems to have been a deeply disturbing event on a very personal level. His physician Lord Moran recalled that many months later, when Allied fortunes were on the upturn, Churchill suddenly and apropos of nothing in particular remarked sadly: 'I cannot get over Singapore'.

PREVIOUS PAGE *Banzai! First days, Singapore 1942* by Ronald Searle, showing jubilant Japanese troops entering the city. Best known as the creator of the St Trinian's School cartoons, Searle was captured at the fall of Singapore while serving with the Royal Engineers and became a prolific visual recorder of the POW experience in South-East Asia.

PREVIOUS PAGE The long road to Bukit Timah: British officers on their way to Yamashita's headquarters at the Ford Motor Factory to negotiate the surrender. Lieutenant General Percival is on the right of the group, Major Cyril Wild on the left with the white flag of truce.

PREVIOUS PAGE Union flag carried by Brigadier Thomas Newbigging, Deputy Adjutant General in Malaya Command, on the way to surrender at Bukit Timah alongside Percival and Wild. The flag was hidden by Wild during his captivity in Changi POW camp and was displayed again when the Japanese surrendered Singapore in September 1945.

After the Battle, Singapore 1942 by Charles Thrale. POWs march into Japanese captivity at Changi, sketched by the artist from a Red Cross truck as he was being taken with them.

No.
Grade No.
General No.
Crime.
Sentence.
Date of Sentence.
Given under my hand and seal of Singapore this
Inspector of Prisons,
S.S. and F.M.S.
Singapore.
AFTER THE BATTLE
1942

CHAPTER FOUR

THE BATTLE FOR HONG KONG

WATSON'S
可口可
SHELTER
PERSONS

ong Kong had been a flourishing trade hub and British colony since 1841. Its largely ethnic Chinese population was governed by a British colonial elite who, alongside Americans and other expatriates, also controlled its economic and financial fortunes. Geopolitically it had always been extremely vulnerable, a tiny appendage of land and associated islands on the south-eastern flank of the colossus that is China. In view of this fact, British military planners simply assumed that Hong Kong was essentially undefendable against a determined attack, and that it was a matter of holding out for as long as possible if only to show willing. In December 1941, Japan's armed forces were in control of the colony's hinterland in China, having captured Canton (Guangzhou) in October 1938 during the early stages of the Second Sino-Japanese War. Hong Kong's fight began on 8 December 1941 when units of the Imperial Japanese Army crossed the Sham Chun (Shenzhen) River into the colony's New Territories.

The Hong Kong Garrison numbered some 14,500 armed personnel and nursing services. British and Indian regular troops were complemented by almost 2,000 Canadian soldiers of the Royal Rifles of Canada and the Winnipeg Grenadiers, collectively known as C Force and commanded by Brigadier John Lawson. There were also local colonial and auxiliary defence units, alongside the Hong Kong Volunteer Defence Corps (HKVDC) which also drew on local European and Chinese manpower. Sea and air defences were pitifully inadequate, the Royal Navy having a few antiquated destroyers and a scattering of other boats, while the RAF had to make do with a handful of old Supermarine Walruses and Vickers Vildebeests. This small air force was effectively destroyed right at the start of the battle for Hong Kong, when the Japanese bombed the airfield at RAF Kai Tak. The event was witnessed by the force's commander, Flight Lieutenant Donald Hill, who recorded his experiences of the first two days in a coded diary:

> Sunday 7/12/41. Much talk about war with Japan but no-one seems to think anything will happen. We, the RAF in Hong Kong, are a very small crowd: seven officers and sixty men with five aircraft, two Walrus and three Vildebeeste...I have the doubtful honour of being [in command] of our

PREVIOUS PAGE Air raid wardens take up position in front of public shelters in Hong Kong during an exercise in the days before the Japanese invasion, as a curious crowd looks on.

Canadian soldiers training on Hong Kong Island before the Japanese invasion. The dispatch of a Canadian force to strengthen the existing garrison was requested by Churchill and agreed to by Canada's Prime Minister William Mackenzie King, in the vain hope that it might help to deter Japanese aggression.

one and only flight...With only five obsolete aircraft and one aerodrome our prospects are not rosy, and it looks as if we might finish up in the army if war comes to Hong Kong.

During the day the news gets worse and all precautions are taken, everyone being confined to camp...Monday 8. I am disturbed early as the Colonial Secretary rings up to say that war with Japan is imminent. Hell, there goes my sleep, and I wake the other officers. Over breakfast we are told that we are at war with Japan. We dash down to flights just in time to hear an ominous roar of planes and nine bombers escorted by over thirty fighters appear heading our way. There's no time to do anything except to man our defence posts. The bombers pass overhead but the fighters swoop down on us and pour a concentrated fire into our planes. We give them all we've got, which is precious little...

After twenty minutes of concentrated attack by the fighters, the Beeste with bombs goes up in smoke and the two Walrus are left blazing and sink. Finally [the Japanese] make off, not unscarred we hope, and we inspect the damage. Both Walrus are gone; one Beeste is ablaze, another badly damaged, leaving one plane intact. We attempt to put out the fire, praying that the bombs won't explode. The blaze is too fierce and she is completely burned, with two red hot heavy bombs among the ruins. One aircraft left but no casualties to personnel... In the afternoon, bombers come over again bombing the docks and Kowloon, one stick [of bombs] dropping on the aerodrome. Heavy fighting reported on the frontier...

Defending that mainland frontier in the New Territories were just three battalions comprising men of the Royal Scots, 14th Punjab and 7th Rajput Regiments, manning the so-called Gin Drinkers' Line. Against overwhelming Japanese forces these men managed to keep a foothold on the New Territories and the Kowloon peninsula for the best part of a week, until the order was given to retreat to Hong Kong Island on 13 December. Donald Hill was already there, having been transformed from an airman into a soldier and engaged in setting up anti-aircraft positions on Bennet's Hill with other RAF personnel:

PREVIOUS PAGE An untitled view of Hong Kong painted by James Morris at the end of the war, while he was working as an official war artist with the British Pacific Fleet.

Muster of officers and NCOs of the Chinese Battalion, Hong Kong Volunteer Defence Corps. The HKVDC originated as a local militia in 1854, in December 1941 it fielded a fighting strength of some 2,200 men and sustained heavy casualties during the battle for Hong Kong Island.

> Sunday fourteenth. Set up positions on Bennetts [sic] and start digging holes in side of hill for billets. Junior and I dig like mad but, owing to rocks, make little progress... Monday fifteenth. Contact Canadians who have positions at foot of Bennetts. They are very helpful bringing us hot tea and helping us in our digging. Am now in the army without a doubt and under the orders of Major Baillee [?] of E Battalion, [Winnipeg] Grenadiers with [headquarters] at Wanchai Gap. More heavy bombing of Aberdeen harbour, heavy casualties to naval personnel caused by explosions of torpedoes and depth charges...
>
> [19 December] Spend half the night pouring rum into semiconscious men who are dead tired after sleepless nights with very little food. We have no reserves and everyone has had a gruelling time. A Canadian sergeant returns to our pillbox at midnight in a state of mental and physical collapse and reports that all his party have been killed. A few hours later another Canadian arrives in a similar condition and with the same story. Worst night I can ever remember, and never was dawn more welcome.

Elsewhere in the colony, Sergeant Lesley Millington was on duty with the Hong Kong Volunteer Defence Corps. The start of his war had been less spectacular than Donald Hill's, as recorded in his diary:

> Monday 8 December: At dawn, two cruisers were seen patrolling up and down outside the range of our guns [at Cape D'Aguilar in the south-east of Hong Kong Island] – they were Japs. At 8am the whole battery was turned out and we were told that we were at war with Japan. Things carried on very much the same as they had done during our many manning exercises except that when a plane came near we took some notice of it. The first plane arrived about noon and made an attack on a small naval patrol vessel which was passing by our battery and missed it with 3 bombs. We could see and hear planes... but we only had one come near us.

Millington's unit was relatively unmolested for a long time, until the Japanese attack on Hong Kong Island began:

> Friday 19 December... At about 10am the master gunner from [the] fire-control post below us came running up and gave orders to blow up our guns and retreat to Stanley Fort, because the Japs had landed on the island the night before and threatened to cut us off. We blew up the guns and destroyed all we could and were beginning to get our kit together when a regular officer came up and told us to leave all excess baggage because we would have to fight our way through to Stanley. Away the [Battalion] went in full fighting order and we arrived in Stanley without seeing one Jap...When we arrived at Stanley Fort we were put to work digging trenches around the peninsula...There were all sorts of people there and all in a confused mass: Canadians, Scots, Middlesex Reg[iment] etc. All had been told to withdraw to Stanley Fort. Nobody knew what to do or when to do it...That night and every night after we manned the trenches we had dug and rested during the day. The Japs were very active bombing and shelling the fort and after a day or so we were quite used to it.

On 18 December the main Japanese invasion force, General Tadayoshi Sano's 38th Division, had launched its assault on Hong Kong Island with landings in strength between North Point and Aldrich Bay. Once more the Japanese made relentless progress against a desperate and ill-coordinated defence, much of the fighting centred on the geographically strategic Wong Nai Chung Gap connecting the northern and southern parts of the island. Once this was in Japanese hands the fall of Hong Kong was only a matter of a short time. In the Bennet's Hill area, Donald Hill was experiencing the disconcerting and demoralising Japanese predilection for night fighting:

> We all carry a good supply of grenades as the Japs are very skilled at getting to close quarters without being spotted. The Jap soldiers wear rubber shoes and are as stealthy as cats. They carry a bag of grenades, automatic weapons,

and light rifle of quarter-inch calibre. They always attack at night and from all directions. Their snipers seem to be everywhere...No one seems to know where the Japs are or how many there are. The High Command, whose daily communiques reveal nothing, seem to know less than anyone else. Chiang Kai-shek's army reported attacking Japs in the rear and we are told to hang on as they will be with us in a few days.

A Japanese landing party advances on Hong Kong Island. Burning oil storage facilities provide a dramatic backdrop, as they did during many other Japanese assaults across the Asia-Pacific theatre of war.

Rumours of Chinese Nationalist forces coming to the rescue were without foundation. Generalissimo Chiang was reluctant to engage with the Japanese at this stage, preferring to conserve his military resources for the coming showdown with his communist enemies within China.

On Christmas Eve Lesley Millington's unit was ordered to move into Stanley village:

I have seen films and pictures of warfare but never in all my life have I seen anything like the sights or heard such a noise as came from Stanley village that night. There were 6 or 7 machine guns of our own, then the Japs' machine guns, rifle fire, tommy guns and the Japs' mortar fire all going on at once and seeming never to stop...

About midnight there was a short lull in the village followed by a terrific row, firing grenades etc, shouting and a weird sort of howl (which I found out later was a sort of Jap war cry). Then the sound of running boots coming along the road towards Harry's gun... I heard Harry shout out and challenge them and they replied that they were friends and not to shoot. Harry let them pass because they were Canadians. The howl came after them towards us and Harry's gun and his crew opened fire along the road. We were all so interested in what was happening on our right that it wasn't until one of the three regulars on our machine gun gave a shout that I saw several figures running towards us across the tennis courts. They were Japs alright because they began to howl. We opened up on them and soon stopped them...

Japanese troops parade through the streets of Hong Kong, 26 December 1941. They are led by Twenty-Third Army commander Lieutenant General Takashi Sakai and Vice Admiral Masaichi Niimi, commander of Japanese naval forces during the battle.

> At about 5am the Japs somehow worked close in under our left flank and threw or fired some sort of incendiary bomb at our magazine. It landed right under the gun and spread over an area of about 16 [square feet] burning like hell and lighting up the whole scene... After about 30 seconds all the ammo in the magazine began to go off all over the place because of the heat.

For the defenders of the island, it was a rapidly losing battle. Just one week after Sano's troops landed, on 25 December – Christmas Day – the Governor of Hong Kong Sir Mark Young and the Commander of British Forces in the colony Major General Christopher Maltby surrendered to Sano's superior, Twenty-Third Army commander Takashi Sakai. He was subsequently appointed Japanese Governor to replace Young and presided over a regime of repression, fear and atrocities. Hong Kong paid a heavy price for its David against Goliath courage.

Under the watchful eye of their Japanese captors, POWs are marched to their designated POW camps four days after the Hong Kong capitulation. Over 10,000 mostly British, Indian and Canadian servicemen went 'into the bag'.

CHAPTER FIVE

THE LONG WAR IN BURMA

British colonial rule in Burma had been established in the 1820s, with the country forming part of British India until it became a separate Crown colony in 1937. The British gave it a limited measure of self-government under a Burmese prime minister. At the start of hostilities with Japan the post was occupied by U Saw, a former lawyer and leader of the nationalist Patriot's Party. In November 1941, U Saw had travelled to London and Washington with a view to persuading both Churchill and Roosevelt that Burma should be granted independence or Dominion status. When it became obvious that Japan was set to become the regional superpower, he initiated contact with Tokyo to secure his own position in Burma should his country be invaded.

An invasion was certainly part of Japan's larger war plan, as Burma would play an important role within the Greater East Asia Co-Prosperity Sphere. The country was rich in oil, timber, rubber, valuable metals and minerals, and was a major grower and exporter of rice. In the short term it would provide a buffer between British India and Japan's conquests further south, and was also the obvious springboard into India itself.

Another important factor in Japanese invasion planning was the existence of the Burma Road – a vital supply route running from the Burmese capital Rangoon (Yangon) via Lashio in north-east Burma to Kunming in south-west China. It had been built in the late 1930s to facilitate Allied supplies to Chiang Kai-shek's forces in the early years of the Second Sino-Japanese War –a function it continued to fulfil, patrolled by aircraft of General Claire Chennault's American Volunteer Group in China, the legendary Flying Tigers. Permanently closing the Burma Road would, it was hoped by the Japanese, severely weaken the Kuomintang government's ability to continue the fight against Japan.

War came to Burma on 14 December 1941, when a special unit of the Japanese 143rd Infantry Regiment, crossing over the border from Thailand, occupied Victoria Point at the southern tip of the country and seized the airfield there. In the following weeks Japanese troops moved up the Kra Isthmus, capturing more airfields around Tenasserim and advancing on Tavoy. On 19 January 1942, two divisions of General Shōjirō Iida's Fifteenth Army and supporting forces attacked out of Thailand

PREVIOUS PAGE Squadron Leader Grant Kerr DFC, flying Spitfires with No.152 Squadron RAF in Burma during 1944–1945. Earlier in the war, Kerr had taken part in operations against the German warships *Scharnhorst*, *Gneisenau* and *Prinz Eugen* during the February 1942 'Channel Dash'.

Two Naga men at Kohima, 1942. Allied forces in the Northeast India-Burma border area benefitted considerably from the Naga's services as auxiliaries including patrolling, intelligence-gathering and ferrying supplies and wounded soldiers through country with which they were intimately familiar.

towards Tavoy, Moulmein and Kawkareik. Their objective was Rangoon, before reaching it they had to overcome the 17th (Indian) Infantry Division commanded by Major General John Smyth, who had the apparent advantage of three rivers – the Salween, Bilin and Sittang (Sittaung) – on which to conduct his defence of the approach to the city. However, superior Japanese force and tactics resulted in a withdrawal to the Sittang, where 'Jackie' Smyth found himself obliged to blow up the vital bridge crossing with most of 17th Division still on the other side. Smyth was dismissed from his command as a result of this controversial episode. On 8 March Rangoon fell to General Sakurai Shōzō's 33rd Division.

The British defence of Burma was arguably not helped by a high command which was apparently confused and subject to a succession of changes. At the time of the Japanese invasion it was the overall responsibility of Wavell's American-British-Dutch-Australian Command (ABDACOM,) having previously been shifted from Far Eastern to India Command.

On the ground, the defence of the country rested with Lieutenant General Thomas Hutton's Burma Army, consisting largely of Indian and Burmese troops who, in a by now sadly familiar tradition, were ill-equipped, poorly trained and no match for the Japanese soldiers they were tasked with repelling. Hutton fell out with Wavell over how the country was to be best defended and was replaced by General Sir Harold Alexander. Hutton experienced the further humiliation of being appointed as Alexander's chief of staff.

The new Burma Army commander failed to hold Rangoon and was himself almost captured by Japanese troops in April 1942 during the battle for the Yenangyaung oilfields. As had happened in Malaya, a general fighting retreat began in the face of increased and determined Japanese forces. Alexander's Burma Army was rapidly losing the fight, despite significant help from two Chinese Nationalist armies further north around Toungoo and Mandalay. In an effort to bring some order into the confusion, a new command known as Burma Corps (Burcorps) was created in mid-March 1942 to rally the scattered British, Indian and Burmese troops. Leadership of Burcorps was entrusted to a veteran of Britain's campaigns in the Middle East, the former commander of 10th Indian

Men of the 7th Rajput Regiment prepare to go out on patrol in the Arakan, 1944. Of the 13 divisions which served as part of Fourteenth Army in Burma, eight were from the Indian Army and contributed decisively to the eventual Allied victory.

Infantry Division Lieutenant General William Slim. It didn't look much like it at the time, but Slim's appointment to Burcorps was to prove a momentous one in the story of British and Allied fortunes in Burma.

While commands and commanders chopped and changed, men on the ground tried to make some sense of what was turning into yet another disaster. Private Neville Hogan, a Karen soldier from Burma, had joined the Burma Auxiliary Force in 1939 and at the time of the Japanese invasion of his country was serving with the Armoured Car Section of the 2nd Battalion Burma Rifles. His first close encounter with the enemy was towards the end of February 1942 on the way south to Moulmein to meet the invaders:

British soldiers patrol the rubble-filled streets of Bahe during the advance on Mandalay in early 1945. In the background the town's pagoda stands largely undamaged.

> On 19 February 1942 (my brother's birthday, which is why I can remember the date) we were ambushed in a roadblock nine miles north of Martaban [Mottama]. The leading car crashed through the roadblock. I was in the second car. We came around the bend in the road to see the enemy, who had been sitting on the trees forming the roadblock, shoot to their feet in surprise. They turned out to be Thai soldiers, forced by the Japs to fight us. We opened fire as did they. They were using small calibre armour-piercing bullets, which came straight through our armour. I was wounded in the right thigh. We were not expecting to be ambushed, as far as we were concerned the war was on the other side of the bay, twelve miles away. Our armoured cars were First World War vintage and the [Thai] bullets jammed the turret, preventing it from training round. We then fought a rearguard action all the way to the Sittang Bridge. We were bombed three times by Blenheim bombers of the RAF, despite standing in the paddy fields waving to them.

Hogan was subsequently among those who found themselves on the wrong side of the bridge when it was blown up on 23 February. He later recalled how:

> ...all hell broke loose as the Japs attacked our position, a settlement around a pagoda. Came down the hill straight at us at first light, with a crackle of fire...We had no telephone, no radios, it was chaos. A private soldier, George Hyde, took command [of Hogan's section], when we were all about to run back across the bridge. We fired at the Japs with our .45 pistols and they were effective, and drove the enemy back. We all said 'this is good' and jumped back into our trenches... When the bridge was blown with us still on the enemy bank I felt devastated and lost...Chaos reigned all that day.

He managed to get across the Sittang on an improvised raft and made his way north to temporary safety.

'Bill' Slim's first task in his new command was the seemingly thankless one of ensuring that Burcorps was able to escape serious losses or even destruction at the hands of Iida's troops.

After the debacle on the Sittang, and the fall of Rangoon, there followed the longest fighting retreat in the history of the British Army – some 1,100 miles through central and northern Burma until Burcorps crossed the border into India in the second half of May 1942. It was an eventful and close-run retreat – with Slim's forces being ordered to attack the Japanese around Prome and Paungde in late March to relieve pressure on the Chinese at Toungoo. This attempt failed, the Chinese abandoned Toungoo and Slim was obliged to continue the retreat to the Yenangyaung oilfields, where heavy fighting occurred in April 1942 amid fires and palls of dense black smoke as oilfield facilities were destroyed to deny them to the Japanese. Burcorps was helped in its fight by soldiers of the Chinese 38th Division, who were ordered from Mandalay and were instrumental in allowing Slim's men to extricate themselves from Yenangyaung before the Japanese took it. Trooper Robert Morris of the 7th Queen's Own Hussars, 7th Armoured Brigade, saw the scene of action on his way north:

> Before we got to the final stage [of the retreat] we had to pass through Yenangyaung, the centre of the Burmese oil industry. I was carrying a load of high-octane petrol and others with trucks full of [ammunition], with flames licking the sides of the vehicles as we drove through. It was keep going or remaining behind and being captured. When we had ferried hundreds of troops back towards the Chindwin [River] we returned and reloaded our normal stores and returned to the Chindwin at Shwegyin. It was hoped that ferry boats would carry the tanks across the river but for lack of crews there weren't enough boats, so the tanks were destroyed... When Burma was recovered the tanks were found where we had left them. We destroyed our trucks as well as throwing ammunition into the river. We were taken to a ferry spot where there were only enough crew for one ferry, but it was big enough to lift large numbers of troops. By then we were all mixed up with soldiers from other units on the other side. The Gurkhas were holding the enemy off.

The Chindwin was the last river crossing before the border with India, not far beyond it were Manipur, Assam and safety.

The major cities of Mandalay and Monywa fell to the Japanese at the beginning of May, shortly after Lashio was captured and the Burma Road cut. The Japanese conquest of Burma was all but completed when Myitkyina in the north-east, near the border with China, was taken on 8 May. The remaining British, Indian, Burmese and Chinese troops withdrew into India not long afterwards.

Burma was now 'liberated' from British colonial control and, it seemed, firmly in Japanese hands. Military planners on both sides got busy devising the next moves. During the summer of 1942, the Japanese worked on plans to capitalise on their success and launch an attack from northern Burma into Assam. A major objective in this undertaking would be

A Gurkha soldier carries a wounded comrade during campaigning in the Arakan. Gurkha troops played a prominent part in operations to clear the Japanese out of Burma in 1944–1945, and in the Chindit Expeditions of 1943 and 1944.

to disrupt the alternative supply route to China, which the Allies had set up following the loss of the Burma Road. Run by the India-China Wing of US Air Transport Command, this was an airlift operation from eastern Assam across part of the Himalayas to Kunming – the original terminus of the Burma Road – the route popularly known among those who flew it as 'the Hump'. On the ground, Wavell – now Commander in Chief India – ordered British forces to launch an offensive from western Assam into north-western Burma towards Akyab (Sittwe) Island in Arakan (Rakhine) State, which was also to be attacked from the sea. The Akyab airfields were considered to be essential to any Allied plan to retake Rangoon. The amphibious assault had to be called off for lack of landing craft, and 14th Indian Division's attempts to advance to Akyab were repulsed with heavy losses. What became known as the First Arakan Campaign, between December 1942 and April 1943, went badly for the British. A two-pronged advance down the Mayu Peninsula towards Donbaik and Akyab, and further inland towards Rathedaung, was halted by strong Japanese resistance, with repeated attempts to take Donbaik and Rathedaung failing. Bill Slim was called to the rescue, assuming command of all forces in the Arakan in mid-April 1943, but his men were too exhausted and weakened further by malaria to make the necessary difference. A month later they were back where they had started the previous December. Conventional ground operations had failed to loosen the Japanese hold on western Burma, but elsewhere in the country other methods were being tried.

In April 1942, as Slim's Burcorps was retreating across Burma, Lieutenant Colonel Orde Wingate arrived in India. He had previously distinguished himself as a proponent and leader of guerrilla-style operations in the 1930s, commanding the Special Night Squads in Palestine as part

Fourteenth Army formation badge, designed by its commander General Sir William Slim. He submitted it anonymously in a competition open to all ranks and collected the £5 prize money awarded for the winning design.

of the British response to the Arab revolt. He then created and commanded Gideon Force to conduct irregular warfare against Benito Mussolini's troops in Ethiopia. Wingate's superior and champion in both roles had been Wavell, and it was Wavell who now called him to action in Burma. Wingate proposed the creation of a long-range penetration force, specialising in jungle warfare, to disrupt Japanese lines of communication and attack their troops wherever they were. The units comprising this force would themselves have no lines of communication, being supplied entirely by air and thus able to move independently through dense jungle and other hostile terrain. The nucleus of this new force was the 77th Indian Infantry Brigade, but it soon became better known as the Chindits – a name derived from the Burmese lion or Chinthe, often seen in sculpted form as guardians of Buddhist temples and monasteries.

'Blood chit' of the type often carried by Allied service personnel, particularly in the Asia-Pacific theatre of war, to be used in the event of the bearer getting into difficulties behind enemy lines. This one is addressed in several languages to 'Dear Friend: I am an Allied fighter. I did not come here to do any harm to you who are my friends. I only want to do harm to the Japanese and chase them away from this country as quickly as possible.'

For a brief period before Burma fell to the Japanese, and before relocating to India, Wingate had been sent to the British-run Bush Warfare School at Maymyo in order to familiarise himself with the basics of his new area of operations, very different from either Palestine or Ethiopia. The commanding officer of the School, Major Michael Calvert, later recalled his first encounter with Wingate and subsequent Chindit training:

> When I got back from the Henzada raid [against Japanese troops in this Irrawaddy River port in March 1942], there was a man sitting at my desk. He got up and said 'I'm Wingate.' I replied 'I'm Calvert and that's my desk.' 'I'm sorry.' I'd never heard of Wingate. He took me for walks; I found that when he talked about guerrilla warfare he was miles ahead of anybody I had met. On arriving in India Wingate sent for me and George Dunlop who had also been fighting in the retreat from Burma. We were both suffering from malnutrition and disease. He said he was forming this brigade and would like us to help, and could I bring as many people from the Bush Warfare School as possible.
>
> Initially members of the staff of the School carried out the training of the brigade... We trained our men in the basing-up

Dear Friend,

I am an Allied fighter. I did not come here to do any harm to you who are my friends. I only want to do harm to the Japanese and chase them away from this country as quickly as possible.

If you will assist me, my Government will sufficiently reward you when the Japanese are driven away.

FRENCH

Cher Ami,

Je suis un combattant allié. Je ne suis pas venu pour vous nuire à vous qui êtes mes amis. Je veux seulement nuire aux Japonais et les chasser de ce pays le plus vite possible.

Si vous voulez m'aider, mon Gouvernement vous récompensera généreusement quand les Japonais seront vaincus.

ANNAMITE

Cùng anh em Việt-Nam yêu dấu,

Tôi là một quân sĩ của đồng-Minh. Tôi tới đây không có mục-đích gì để phá hại dân chúng Annam là bạn thân của tôi. Tôi chỉ muốn phá hại quân Nhật và đuổi chúng nó ra Khỏi Đông—Dương cho đặng mau chóng. Nếu các anh có thể dẫn đường cho tôi đi tới gần nơi trại binh của Đồng-Minh; thì Chánh-Phủ của tôi sẽ ban thưởng cho cac anh một cách rất xứng đáng.

MALAY

Kawan,

Saya askar pehak benkat saya tida datung sini besat bekin soesa sama kita orang. Orang Sumatra (Malay) punia kawan saya mow… sama orang djepan … dari negri lakas k… tidak saja … saja, orang Sumatra. … saja berperang sehingga Djepoen sadja saja berperang sehingga di-oesir dari negeri Melajoe ini. Kalau tolong saja, kerajaan saja tentu membalas boedi toean dengan tjoekoep la-itoe bila orang Djepoen itu habis di-halau.

HAKA

Ka Koi,

Kema ne Mirang … Zangfak on, nangma … a um nak lam nai byik a nang ka kalpi a … a-so-za ne laksawng a tam pi pek lai.

KACHIN

Khau Du ni,

Ngai gaw Ingalit hypenma rai nga ai. Anhte gaw nanhte hpe aru ara jaw na matu sa n rai. Alawan Japanni hpe Myenmung kaw na shachynt kau na matu sa ni ai.

Khauni anhte Khau hpyenmani dap de gadum ai lam kaw na shangun dat yang, gumhpraw sungui asoyani law law jaw na ra ai.

LAIZO

Ka Rual,

Keimah in Mirang ralkap kasi. Hinah nanmah zonzai peek dingah ka ra lo. Rualpi tha nan si. Japan ral hi zonzai peek ih, nan khua ram in zamtang ten dawi hlo ka duh.

Kanmah Mirang le Amerikan ralkap pawl um nak a nai bik ah zangfah ten in feh pi le, ka bawi pawl in laksawng tha a lo pe ding.

KAREN

TAMIL

W. SHAN

E. SHAN AND N. THAI

CHINESE

我是一位同盟國的戰鬥員。馬來亞的民眾都是我的朋友。我決不會來傷害你們的。我的目的是要消滅日本軍隊，或是把他們驅逐出境。若是你們能幫助我，等我們打敗日本以後，政府一定會重賞你們。

BURMESE

BENGALI

or bivouacking drills that would become a daily feature of life on Chindit operations. As the column approached the end of the day's march, the column commander would be near the front and he would find a suitable place. You couldn't hesitate for long with four hundred or so men behind you. Some of the essentials were water and bamboo to feed the mules [used as pack animals]. Provided it was possible to combine it with water, we would try to find a place with fairly high ground so our signal sets would carry the two hundred miles back to India. We would set up a defensive position off the path while the rearguard marched on as a deception before brushing away the footprints and setting up an ambush to catch any Japanese following up... The men would go to fill their water bottles. The upper piece of the stream was for water bottles, the next piece for mules, then for washing and the lowest for defecating. We always tried to use running water for latrines, so it would be washed away and not give away our position.

Orde Wingate (left) and William Slim. The Fourteenth Army commander feared he was losing some of his best fighting units to the Chindits and was not convinced of the strategic value of Wingate's operations.

Calvert was one of many who thought highly of Wingate's approach to fighting the Japanese, and of the Chindit ethos:

Underlying all the training was Wingate's firm belief that his Long-Range Penetration Force would outdo the Japanese. I don't want to be too hard on the British and Indian armies at the time, but they were to a large extent demoralised, they thought that the Jap was invincible. There were well-meaning posters up all over India showing cruel Japanese bayoneting children. Instead of making people want to fight the Japanese it made them frightened. We had to build up the morale of the British to remember they were tough. I think this was why Wingate said that beards would be allowed. I personally would not allow mournful beards. I insisted that we should have aggressive beards, like conquistadores.

Wingate inspired great admiration and loyalty in many of the men he led. Private Charles Aves of the 13th Battalion King's Regiment (Liverpool) was one of these:

> [Wingate] came to see us in Secunderabad and addressed us. He created a great effect on most of us. I felt I was in the presence of somebody really extraordinary, the type of person I had never come across before. He exuded an aura of power. And yet he didn't speak in that manner, he spoke quietly and convincingly... He realigned our perception of what was possible for ordinary people like ourselves. He lifted us. We were left realising that our cushy life in India was coming to an end. He told us we were in for a very hard time training. We were going to show the Japanese we could do better. We were in awe of him. He convinced us that we could do it. He was a great man.

Major Stanisław Lisiecki, a Polish officer of the 1st Battalion, Gambia Regiment talking with one of his men (whose name was not recorded) in Burma in June 1945. The original photograph caption states that there were over 100,000 West Africans serving in India and Burma at that time.

Many others saw him differently. His often eccentric personal habits, short temper and abrasive manner turned some people against him. Fellow officers, in particular, could find him difficult to deal with, to the extent that not a few of them came to the conclusion that he was mentally unbalanced, if not insane. Whatever manner of man he was, Wingate's leadership and fighting philosophy were soon put to the test against the Japanese forces in Burma.

The First Chindit Expedition, codenamed 'Longcloth', was launched in mid-February 1943, with the principal objective of cutting several vital transport and supply routes in a large area between Mandalay and Myitkyina. It was also meant to show the Japanese that their opponents could strike them anywhere and at will, with a consequent unsettling and demoralising effect. The operation was only partially successful. Some infrastructure was destroyed and routes cut but the Chindits found that the sparse nature of much of the jungle in that part of Burma was not as conducive to guerrilla tactics as had been expected. The Japanese reacted swiftly and efficiently to the incursions, and, by the end of March, Wingate was already planning a withdrawal back across the Chindwin. At the time, a War Office report on 'Longcloth' judged it to have been of no strategic value, reinforcing the negative views of many who considered Wingate and his Chindits to be more of a liability than an asset. But for others the operation confirmed the potential benefits of irregular warfare, albeit imperfectly carried out on this occasion, as well as a valuable

means of gathering intelligence and boosting morale. For public consumption the expedition was heralded as a victory. Expecting to be taken to task for not having achieved more, Wingate was instead feted as the man of the hour – not least by Churchill, who took him along to the Anglo-American Quebec Conference in August 1943 to sing the praises of the plucky Chindits. The result of this endorsement at the highest level was a considerable expansion of the Chindit force. The original 77th Indian Infantry Brigade was joined by Brigadier Walter Lentaigne's 111th Indian Infantry Brigade, the British 70th Division and elements of the 81st (West African) Division.

Duly impressed with Wingate, and not wanting to be outdone by the British in long-range penetration operations, the Americans created their own Chindit equivalent, the

unremarkably named 5307th Composite Unit (Provisional). The new unit was commanded by Brigadier General Frank Merrill and soon became more popularly known as 'Merrill's Marauders'. They operated largely independently of the Chindits, after initial attempts to put them under Wingate's control were resisted by the senior US commander in the China-Burma-India theatre, General Joseph Stilwell. When he learned of this decision, Wingate was livid and exclaimed that Stilwell could 'stick his Americans up his arse'. During their relatively short operational history in Burma, Merrill's men gave as good an account of themselves as any Chindit, particularly in what proved to be their swansong, the recapture of Myitkyina in August 1944.

Meanwhile, the substantially augmented Chindit force was given another opportunity to show what it could do, in the Second Chindit Expedition, codenamed 'Thursday', which commenced in February 1944. The main objectives were to capture Japanese airfields at Indaw and disrupt lines of communication between Myitkyina, Mandalay and Bhamo as part of a larger Anglo-American offensive in northern Burma, in concert with Stilwell's Chinese forces and Merrill's Marauders. Initial operations went well for the Chindits but the most significant event for them was a tragedy. On 24 March 1944, Wingate was returning by air from Burma to India when the aircraft he was in crashed in the jungle-covered hills of Manipur, killing all on board. It was a body blow from which the force never recovered. Its leadership passed to Walter 'Joe' Lentaigne, and, to the chagrin of many Chindits, overall command of the force was then transferred to Stilwell. Wingate would surely have been horrified.

During the course of their operations the Chindits had acquired a wealth of intelligence about the character and mindset of their Japanese adversaries in Burma. Before the force was finally disbanded in February 1945, it distilled some of this knowledge into a document titled *Through Japanese Eyes*, for the benefit and entertainment of others who sought to 'know your enemy'. Based largely on captured Japanese personal diaries and other documents, it aimed to reveal the men behind the masks. As the introduction stated:

PREVIOUS PAGE Sierra Leonian soldiers of the 81st (West African) Division with a Japanese rifle and helmets captured during the Second Arakan Campaign, 1943–1944, in which the division played a significant part.

> A soldier's knowledge of his enemy is generally rudimentary. Generally he is referred to as 'the bloody Jap', or worse, and it is never realised the enemy is just another man. For a long time this ignorance was serious and the 'invincible Japanese' myth grew out of it. Battle, however, dispersed much of this nonsense and there was nothing as salutary as the sight of fat Japanese buttocks wobbling away from the approaching flame throwers to bring the matter to its true perspective. At the same time, you learned to respect his endurance, his wiliness, his ability to dig himself in, and his courage as shown at Mogaung where a solitary private took on eight officers all armed with carbines...[It] is only when you really understand your enemy in every degree, that you can go in with confidence and beat him.

By the time of Wingate's death the war in Burma was reaching a crucial turning-point in the Allies' favour, enabling them to 'go in with confidence' as they had not done before. In January 1944, General Philip Christison's XV Indian Corps had launched an offensive into the Arakan, in another attempt to recapture Akyab via Maungdaw. The Japanese counter-attacked and a fierce battle developed around Christison's main supply and command base at Sinzweya, known as the Admin Box. Although they achieved initial successes, the Japanese could not take the Box in face of tenacious defence, superior artillery and air power, including airborne resupply, and tanks. Towards the end of February the Japanese operations were called off, the first major defeat for them in Burma since the war began. As it turned out it was the beginning of the end. Closely following on the battle for the prosaically named, and now largely forgotten, Admin Box, two more battles took place which achieved far greater fame and resonance in the record of British military actions in Burma.

In March 1943, command of the Japanese Fifteenth Army had been transferred from Shōjirō Iida to Lieutenant General Renya Mutaguchi, a veteran of the campaigns in Malaya, Singapore and the Philippines. A year later, he was finally authorised to carry out his long-planned and personally cherished offensive into Northeast India, codenamed *U-Go*. Its immediate objectives were the British supply bases at

THROUGH JAPANESE EYES

THIS DOCUMENT
MUST NOT FALL
INTO
ENEMY HANDS

Imphal and Kohima, and beyond Kohima the major railhead at Dimapur. Imphal was the most important base and the main objective, but control of the supply and communications route from Imphal through Kohima to Dimapur was crucial to Japanese success. Capturing these objectives would cripple further British-led offensives in northern Burma as well as disrupting Allied air and ground supply routes into China. Mutaguchi also entertained visions of spearheading a more general invasion of India, leading to the collapse of British rule. This exalted objective was reflected in the words of an 'Order of the Day' of early February 1944, which later fell into Chindit hands and was reproduced in *Through Japanese Eyes*:

Through Japanese Eyes, the 1945 Chindit guide to the mentality and modus operandi of the Japanese soldier.

> At this time when the World War is rapidly reaching its climax and our attack and defence have suddenly become violent, our Burma Occupational Unit has been given the great honour of invading INDIA. Ours is a great honour which cannot be surpassed. Finally, after having built ourselves up spiritually and physically with much impatience, we have come to the point of decisive action... As the nucleus of the entire front in the Burma operations, our infantry will crash through the INDO-BURMA border and will be in control of the enemy's fate.

Directing the defence of Imphal and Kohima was Bill Slim, who had been in command of the newly-created Fourteenth Army – the successor to what had previously been known as Eastern Army – since November 1943. From the beginning of March until well into June, an epic struggle was waged for the Imphal-Kohima-Dimapur area. Conditions came to resemble those on the Western Front during the First World War, with blasted landscapes, desperate close quarters fighting and attritional warfare. Some flavour of conditions at Kohima was given in a later interview by Benjamin 'Tom' Cattle, a Private in the 2nd Battalion Dorsetshire Regiment, who found himself on the key Garrison Hill position:

> We were now taking heavy casualties on Garrison Hill... The only way up was on the road in carriers to a place called Mortuary Corner. Anything approaching this point came

Men and mules of a Chindit column crossing a river during the Second Chindit Expedition ('Thursday') in May 1944.

The remains of Scraggy Hill after fierce fighting at Imphal in April 1944. Men of the 3rd Battalion, 10th Gurkha Rifles paid a particularly heavy price in casualties for denying it to the Japanese.

Burmese Guerrillas in Action (1945) by Leslie Cole. In Burma, as elsewhere in South-East Asia, indigenous anti-Japanese resistance and guerrilla organisations were encouraged and supplied by Britain's Special Operations Executive (SOE), operating in the region as Force 136.

under Jap mortar and artillery fire... From the road Garrison Hill was almost perpendicular, the monsoon had started early and every step you tried to pull yourself up you slid back with all your kit. At the same time being sniped at, machine-gunned and mortared and shelled. We got to the top and were given our positions, the original positions dug by the Royal West Kents. There were bodies lying around. We scrambled into a slit [trench]... There was only enough room for three of us, about eight feet long, two feet wide with a roof on it... You couldn't get out of your trench in daylight or the Japanese snipers would have you. So many shells and mortar bombs had hit the hill that all the trees were shattered and the stumps were draped with parachutes that had come down with supplies. It was a desolate and desperate situation.

A hunting horn used by Captain John Lawrence Smyth of C Company, 1st Battalion, Queen's Royal Regiment to rally his men in battle. The horn was retrieved after his death in action at Kohima in May 1944 and given to his father, Brigadier Sir John 'Jackie' Smyth.

Water was dropped in two-gallon cans. We were connected trench to trench by ropes so we could pull supplies, water cans and ammunition across from one trench to another. On one occasion we were pulling a water can to our trench and it got caught on the stump of a tree, and we couldn't move it. And Des the Lance Corporal said 'I'll have a look and see'.

> He stood up and fell back, shot dead straight through the forehead. He had to stay in the trench with us until dark. He was such a nice chap and we'd been together for such a long time.

As Cattle's story suggests, supply by air played a crucial role in the Fourteenth Army's ultimate victory at Imphal and Kohima. The RAF ensured that the supplies were dropped where they were needed, while its Third Tactical Air Force inflicted severe punishment on Japanese forces on the ground. Mutaguchi had gambled on being able to take Imphal, Kohima and Dimapur quickly and without having to bring up substantial reinforcements through difficult jungle terrain. His gamble failed, at a terrible cost of around 60,000 casualties. British and Indian losses were substantially less, but the suffering had been just as great. In July 1944, the *U-Go* offensive was finally called off and Mutaguchi's dream of leading a Japanese victory parade in Delhi evaporated. For Slim and his Fourteenth Army veterans it was the start of the long road back to Rangoon and the conclusion of a war that did not end until late August 1945, when Japanese forces in Burma officially surrendered – 13 days after 'Victory over Japan' (VJ) Day. Many battles still lay ahead and many lives would still be lost, but the tide had been decisively turned.

CHAPTER SIX

WAR IN THE PACIFIC

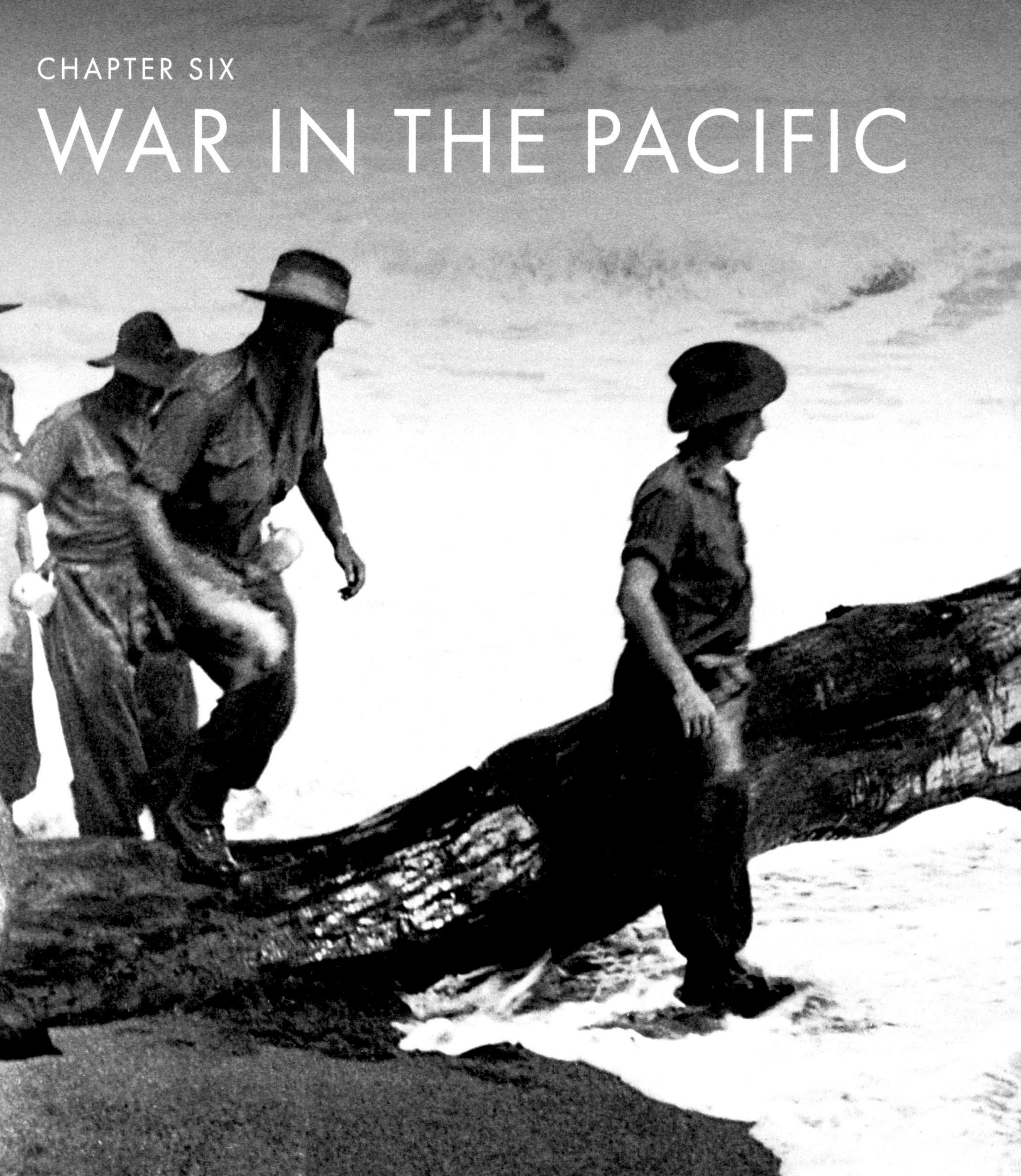

December 1941 was a busy month for Japan's armed forces. The attacks on Pearl Harbor, Malaya, Hong Kong and southern Burma were just a few of the items on their agenda. On 9 December they landed on Makin and Tarawa in the Gilbert and Ellice Islands (now Kiribati and Tuvalu) – a British colonial possession – halfway between Hawaii and New Guinea. Along with the Marshall and Mariana Islands, these formed a natural defensive perimeter to the south-east of the Greater East Asia Co-Prosperity Sphere. Japan reinforced this perimeter by occupying the US Pacific bases of Guam and Wake Island later in the month. The other main prizes to the west were the Philippine Islands and the Dutch East Indies, together with Dutch and Australian New Guinea, the Bismarck Archipelago and the Solomon Islands to the south. Just beyond these lay Australia itself.

Comprising over 7,000 islands and islets across a vast area between Taiwan and Borneo, the Philippines posed a considerable challenge to the main Japanese Fourteenth Army invasion force which landed on the principal northern island of Luzon on 22 December. Commanding this Army was General Masaharu Homma, who was ordered to capture the Philippine capital Manila within 50 days of the initial landings. Homma was not one to take what he considered to be unreasonable orders lying down and had got into an argument with his superiors, who blithely informed him that the US-Filipino forces opposing him were 'third class and unworthy to face us in battle'.

These supposedly inferior troops were General Douglas MacArthur's US Army Forces in the Far East. Their defence of Luzon had already been dealt a serious blow by devastating Japanese attacks on the main US air bases at Clark Field and elsewhere on the island on 8 December and over subsequent days. MacArthur and his senior commander in the Philippines, Major General Jonathan Wainwright, were unable to stem the Japanese onslaught. A fighting retreat down the length of Luzon ended in the Bataan Peninsula to the west of Manila, which MacArthur declared an open city to spare it the worst, with the Philippine government and MacArthur's headquarters evacuating to the island fortress of Corregidor in Manila Bay. MacArthur's demands to Washington for reinforcements and

PREVIOUS PAGE Australian soldiers advance on Salamaua in New Guinea, 1943. All who had to fight in this jungle-covered and malaria-infested island faced enormous challenges in one of the most arduous campaigns of the war.

Roosevelt flanked by his top Pacific commanders General Douglas MacArthur and Admiral Chester Nimitz. MacArthur often came across as an overbearing self-publicist who wanted the glory for himself, whereas Nimitz tended to leave the headlines to others.

assistance were not met, and his troops were left to hold out for as long as they could. This heroically futile undertaking was immortalised in popular verse of the time:

> We're the battling bastards of Bataan,
> No mama, no papa, no Uncle Sam,
> No aunts, no uncles, no cousins, no nieces,
> No pills, no planes or artillery pieces,
> And nobody gives a damn!

Wainwright's men finally conceded defeat in early April 1942. Corregidor held out a month longer but Roosevelt ordered MacArthur to leave the island on 12 March and relocate his headquarters to Australia, with the General famously promising: 'I shall return'. Over 70,000 American and Filipino troops were captured by the Japanese on Bataan, but they had another ordeal to undergo in a gruelling trek to their designated POW camps, which became known as the Bataan Death March. Many hundreds of US and thousands of Filipino servicemen perished as a result of this war crime. With further landings on the main southern island of Mindanao and others in between, the Philippines were firmly in Japanese hands.

Events in the Dutch East Indies (now mostly within modern-day Indonesia) moved just as rapidly around the same time. The British were in fact the first casualties, as the campaign opened on 16 December 1941 with Japanese landings in Brunei and Sarawak in British Borneo. North Borneo was taken in January 1942, completing the capture of British possessions on the island – the rest of Borneo was Dutch. To secure the abundant natural resources of the Dutch East Indies, its oil above all, as quickly as possible, General Hitoshi Imamura's Sixteenth Army was directed to land at key points in Dutch Borneo, the Celebes and the Moluccas in mid-December 1941, followed by landings in Sumatra and Timor. Wavell's ABDACOM was tasked with co-ordinating the defence of the Dutch East Indies from its headquarters in Java. However, Allied forces were overwhelmed and outmanoeuvred by the Japanese airborne and amphibious assaults. ABDACOM's naval force, commanded by Dutch Admiral Karel Doorman,

A Japanese snapshot of the Bataan Death March, April 1942. It conveys nothing of the horrors of this event, which contributed to the post-war death sentence passed by the Allies on General Masaharu Homma, commander of the Japanese Fourteenth Army during the 1941–1942 Philippines campaign.

attempted to protect Bali and Java from Japan's invasion fleets, culminating in the Battle of the Java Sea on 27 February 1942, but to no avail. The Allied force was all but destroyed and Doorman went down with his flagship *De Ruyter*. Wavell was compelled to relocate to India ahead of the impending Japanese invasion of Java, and his ill-starred American-British-Dutch-Australian Command was dissolved.

The last days before the capitulation in Java were experienced by Captain Andrew Duncan of the 2nd Argyll and Sutherland Highlanders, attached to Wavell's headquarters at Lembang at the time it was disbanded:

> Files were being burned, documents and equipment packed, officers were trying to get their effects together, arms and ammunition were being issued and, of course, the usual orders, counter-orders and disorder. Lieutenant Des Campion and self maintained an aloof air to all this, as on the previous evening we had volunteered to stay behind, but nevertheless, deep down, felt rather envious and wondered exactly what the future held for us...
>
> Later when my car (bought for one guilder) had been loaded with stores, kit and tommy gun we departed from Lembang to take up our duties under General Sitwell [Major General Hervey Sitwell, General Officer Commanding British Troops in Java]. The few peaceful remaining days were a Godsend after the hectic time we had experienced at Lembang...
>
> The days quickly passed and we were wondering if the blow would fall, when one day Colonel Dobbin came over to our office and told us that a large number of Japanese naval and

Royal Netherlands East Indies Army (KNIL) sleeve patch. Over 90,000 KNIL personnel surrendered to the Japanese in March 1942. Their commander, General Hein ter Poorten, cited the 'impossibility of protecting them from the enemy's air attacks' as a crucial factor in their defeat.

> transport ships had been sighted steaming towards Java and that although the Dutch Navy and Air Force were attending to this matter we would have to expect invasion within three days – I might add here that the Dutch Navy in conjunction with British Naval units gave an extremely good account of themselves, but unfortunately were almost entirely wiped out due to overwhelming odds, whilst right up to the capitulation, the Dutch and British Air Forces hammered away at the enemy though their numbers had dwindled away to practically nothing.

Duncan was in the Bandoeng (Bandung) area when the invasion came on 1 March:

> One of the most amazing sights I have ever seen was the effect of the sounding of the air raid siren in Bandoeng... What had a few minutes before been a township full of bustle and laughter, became a place devoid of movement and sound save for scurrying footsteps of some tardy Dutchman seeking refuge. Cafes and shops closed their doors and for those of us who preferred to remain in the open Bandoeng presented a vista of deserted streets...
>
> From reports received at headquarters, it became increasingly obvious that the situation was rapidly becoming critical as the Japanese were progressing steadily and the strength of our air force, from the very start hopelessly inadequate, was rapidly diminishing... I had in my charge at that time documents of such a nature that it was imperative that they did not fall into the hands of the enemy so, in order that their complete destruction might be carried out, I had requested adequate warning of the approach of the Japanese. The invasion of Java had taken place on Sunday March 1 and on the following Thursday Colonel Dobbin... came strolling across from his office, the eternal pipe in his mouth, and announced in the most casual manner 'Oh Duncan, I thought you might be interested to know that the Japs are quite close'. Upon my enquiring just how close, he replied 'Oh about 12 miles up the road', and with that walked away...

A Japanese soldier looks on as oil storage tanks burn at Tandjong (Tanjung) Priok in northern Java, February 1942. Access to its oil resources was the main driver of the Japanese invasion of the Dutch East Indies.

Duncan spent the next few days evading the advancing Japanese and planning his escape from the island, first by aircraft and then when that proved impossible, by boat. His attempts, along with those of many other Allied servicemen, came to nothing and he found himself 'in the bag' as a POW at Tandjong (Tanjung) Priok in Batavia (Jakarta). The island was surrendered to Imamura's forces on 8 March by the Commander in Chief of the Royal Netherlands East Indies Army and de facto head of Allied forces in Java, General Hein ter Poorten. The Dutch East Indies were added to Japan's victory tally.

Following his relocation from the Philippines to Australia, Douglas MacArthur was appointed to a new command in April 1942, South West Pacific Area (SWPA). This effectively replaced ABDACOM and comprised the general area of the Philippines, Borneo, Dutch East Indies, New Guinea, Australia and the Western Solomon Islands. Much of this region was under Japanese occupation and MacArthur's longer-term task was to take it back. The vast expanse of the Pacific to the east of SWPA was the domain of the navy, entrusted to Kimmel's successor as Commander in Chief of the US Pacific Fleet, Admiral Chester Nimitz. His new command was named Pacific Ocean Areas. Their immediate concern was to prevent or counter further Japanese offensives in the south and central Pacific, as its military leaders showed no signs of resting on their laurels.

Japan's next moves seemed to pose an imminent threat to Australia itself. During March, April and May 1942 its forces landed on both Dutch and Australian New Guinea, the Bismarck Archipelago and Tulagi in the Solomon Islands. In mid-February Japanese bombers had already hit the city of Darwin on Australia's north coast, and did so again a month later, prompting the Australian government to draw up plans to conduct a 'scorched earth'-type retreat in the event of an invasion of the country. In Australian New Guinea (Papua) the Japanese planned to capture the capital, Port Moresby, from which to expand their operations. This objective was, however, frustrated in early May at the Battle of the Coral Sea, the first major naval action in history involving aircraft carriers. On the Allied side it was conducted by a combined US-Australian force

USMC
42777

led by Admiral Frank Fletcher. On the face if it the battle was a victory for the Japanese, who sank the carrier USS *Lexington*, but Fletcher had inflicted enough damage on his opponents for the Port Moresby operation to be called off. The Japanese never quite recovered from this setback, which at long last gave the Allies some reasons for hope.

There were other signs that the Japanese were not having things all their own way. On 18 April 1942, US Army Air Force B-25 bombers took off from the carrier USS *Hornet*, 700 miles east of Tokyo, led by Colonel James Doolittle. The cities of Tokyo, Kobe, Nagoya, Yokosuka and Yokohama were all hit. The operation cost the Americans dearly as most of the bombers subsequently had to crash-land in Chinese territory and casualties were high, but the Doolittle Raid was in other respects an important morale-booster for the Allies. It also demonstrated to the Japanese leadership that their homelands were by no means invulnerable to Allied attack – although most of the civilian population seem to have thought it was an elaborate air raid exercise.

The first significant turning-point of the war in the Allies' favour came in early June 1942. Ever since Pearl Harbor the Commander in Chief of the Japanese Combined Fleet, Admiral Yamamoto, had been looking for an opportunity to lure the US Pacific Fleet into a decisive battle that would result in its final destruction. The strategically placed US outpost of Midway Atoll, between Hawaii and Japan, seemed to offer the perfect arena for such an engagement, and Yamamoto laid his plans for Operation *Mi*. An attack on Midway would, it was hoped, draw the main body of the US fleet into battle there, while a diversionary attack on the Aleutian Islands to the north, just off the south-west coast of mainland Alaska, would split Nimitz' forces. Unfortunately for Yamamoto, his American opposite number knew about the Midway-Aleutians operation before it happened, thanks to US naval intelligence's ability to read the Japanese JN-25 naval operational code. Nimitz declined the Aleutians bait, enabling a token Japanese occupation of Attu and Kiska, and concentrated two Task Forces on Midway, led by Admirals Frank Fletcher and Raymond Spruance. They faced an apparently superior force, or three separate forces, led by Admirals Yamamoto, Nagumo and Kondō, but now it was

US Marines emerge from the jungle of Guadalcanal after the defeat of Japanese forces there in January 1943. In a remarkable rescue operation by the Imperial Japanese Navy, over 13,000 Japanese survivors got away from the island unhindered by the Americans, but they left 25,000 dead behind them after five months of desperate fighting.

PREVIOUS PAGE Midway, June 1942. The aircraft carrier USS *Yorktown*, Admiral Frank Fletcher's flagship, receives a direct hit from a Japanese aerial torpedo. *Yorktown* was mortally wounded during the first day of the battle, but it took three more days for her to sink.

the Americans who demonstrated the superior tactics. Their torpedo and dive-bombers wreaked havoc among the Japanese, taking all four of Nagumo's 1st Carrier Striking Force aircraft carriers out of action. It was a devastating blow to Japan's naval power in the Pacific, shifting the balance decisively towards the Allies.

To exploit the favourable conditions created by the Midway victory, MacArthur and Nimitz were tasked with evicting the Japanese from the Solomon Islands and the Bismarck Archipelago. The primary aim was to neutralise the key Japanese base at Rabaul on New Britain. An offensive in Papua-New Guinea was also planned to facilitate this objective, thus removing the threat to Australia and securing the vital maritime supply lanes in the area. The initial focus of the Solomons campaign was the island of Guadalcanal and the capture of the Japanese airfield there. The amphibious landings on 7 August 1942 and the subsequent operations on Guadalcanal were carried out by Major General Alexander Vandergrift's US 1st Marine Division, supported at sea by Frank Fletcher's Task Force 61. Intense heat, poisonous insects and snakes, malaria-bearing mosquitos and often impenetrable vegetation made the island a challenging environment at the best of times. For both Japanese and American soldiers, it became a 'green hell' for six long months until Guadalcanal was finally secured in February 1943.

Conditions in the Australian territories of Papua and New Guinea were equally challenging, and the fight for the eastern end of the main island, nearest the Solomons and New Britain, lasted from July 1942 to January 1943. The Australian 7th Division commanded by Generals Arthur 'Tubby' Allen and then George Vasey carried a major part of the burden of battle, sustaining heavy casualties, not least from malaria and other tropical diseases. The Japanese fared even worse, in some cases resorting to cannibalism to avoid death by starvation as their supplies ran out. Some idea of conditions in New Guinea is conveyed by Australian veteran Reginald Bandy, who served there with 43rd Landing Craft Company:

> You get to New Guinea and there's nothing; there's mosquitos, there's snakes, there's leeches and it rains every

> day and you're wet all the time... The jungle was very thick and the hills were very high, and in those days the wirelesses that everybody had weren't too hot... When you're in the jungle you can only see about ten feet... The Japanese used to do a lot of fighting at night ... they'd crawl up to within five or six metres of your pit and tie a piece of string or rope to a bush and go back twenty or thirty metres and keep pulling this, and all they want you to do is fire a shot...You've got to lie there all night and every five or ten minutes this thing's rattling, you've got to put in the back of your mind that there's no one there. For Christ's sake don't fire or you're dead.

Japanese naval flag captured by US infantry at Cape Gloucester, New Britain (Bismarck Archipelago), in January 1944. They were taking part in the joint US-Australian Operation 'Cartwheel' during 1943–1944 to neutralise the major Japanese base at Rabaul.

American and Australian progress in the Pacific continued slowly but surely through 1943. In the north the Aleutians were retaken, the Japanese were pushed out of most of the Solomons, concentrating their defence on Bougainville Island, and in New Guinea and the Bismarck Archipelago efforts to isolate Rabaul were bearing fruit. Bougainville was the scene of a small but significant incident in April 1943, when the Americans' reading of Japanese naval codes resulted in US fighters shooting down the aircraft carrying Admiral Yamamoto on a tour of inspection. It was a grievous loss for

the Japanese and for the Americans a more personal settling of scores for Pearl Harbor. In November 1943, the Americans began their so-called 'island-hopping' or 'leapfrogging' campaign towards the Philippines and, ultimately, Japan with amphibious landings on Makin and Tarawa in the Gilbert Islands. The Marshalls followed in January–February 1944 with landings on Kwajalein and Eniwetok Attols. During June and July Saipan, Tinian and Guam in the Marianas fell to the US Marines, by which time MacArthur had finally secured enough of New Guinea to free up American troops for the assault on the Philippines. At sea the Japanese Navy suffered another serious defeat in the Battle of the Philippine Sea in June 1944, popularly referred to by the victors as 'The Great Marianas Turkey Shoot'. What began at Midway had developed into a painstaking, necessarily piecemeal, but nonetheless relentless Allied encroachment on Japan's core territories, and Japan's leaders were forced to contemplate the previously unthinkable: that the war might be lost.

A group of South Pacific Scouts in New Georgia (Solomon Islands) in 1944. Specialists in jungle warfare, the Scouts were recruited primarily in Fiji and the Solomons and were led by white officers, mainly from New Zealand.

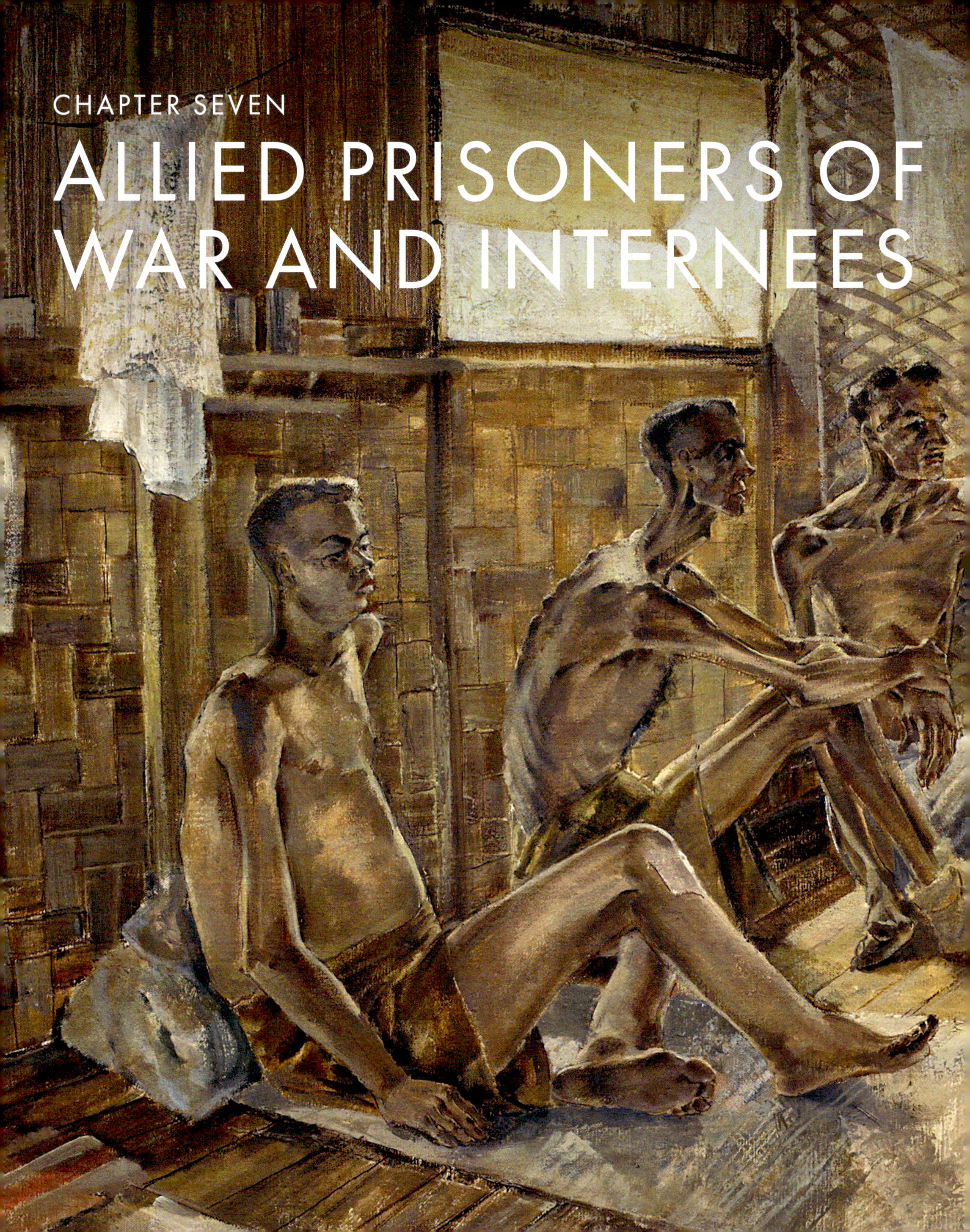

CHAPTER SEVEN

ALLIED PRISONERS OF WAR AND INTERNEES

It is difficult to estimate the total number of POWs who fell into Japanese hands from December 1941 onwards. Around 350,000 is a widely accepted – although likely a very conservative – figure, of which a considerable proportion were service personnel from the USA, Netherlands / Dutch East Indies and from Britain, its Empire and Commonwealth. The majority of the rest were Chinese. For the Japanese serviceman, being taken POW was a disgrace and proof of shameful cowardice. His view of non-Japanese POWs was shaped accordingly. They were beneath contempt and had forfeited their right to humane treatment. This was compounded by the brutal discipline enforced within the Imperial Japanese Army, which was extended to those it captured in battle. Many thousands of Allied POWs taken in the first flush of Japanese victory soon found out just how little their lives were valued by their captors.

The early days of captivity generally gave few indications of things to come. Having taken such a large haul of prisoners within a short time, the Japanese very often seemed in no hurry to do anything with them. In Java, having failed to find a means of escape by sea or air, Andrew Duncan and his comrades enjoyed what he later humorously termed a 'seaside holiday':

> We left the aerodrome and proceeded to the nearby beach where we found a small community of fellow would-be escapees sporting themselves in the sea clad in their birthday suits so lost no time in joining them... Time quickly passed as our days were spent in bathing, fishing and shopping expeditions to the village where we haggled with natives over the prices of chicken, sugar, eggs, fruit and sarongs.

It was several weeks before this apparent idyll was abruptly ended, with what Duncan called 'the rude awakening' of being transported to the Tandjong Priok POW camp at Batavia where very different conditions prevailed.

In Hong Kong, Flight Lieutenant Donald Hill had also attempted escape with equal lack of success. His truck was commandeered by Japanese officers who treated him as their driver in a surreal interval between capitulation and captivity:

PREVIOUS PAGE *Orderly on his Rounds in X Ward, Changi Gaol, Singapore, with POWs suffering from Starvation and Beriberi* (1945) by Leslie Cole.

Overcrowded and insanitary conditions in Changi Prison, Singapore, which at different times during the war housed both POWs and civilian internees.

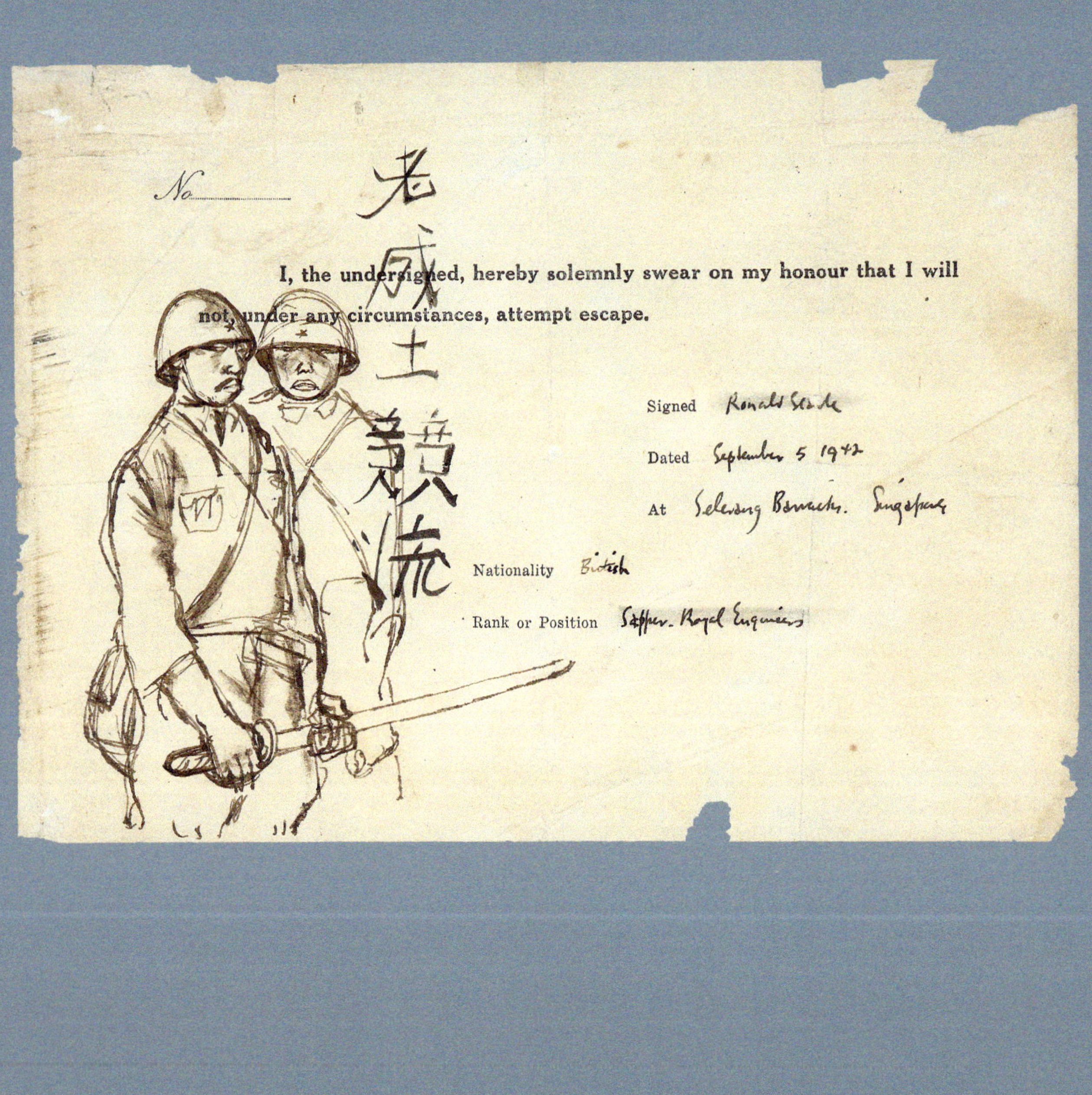

No.

I, the undersigned, hereby solemnly swear on my honour that I will not, under any circumstances, attempt escape.

Signed Ronald Searle

Dated September 5 1942

At Selarang Barracks. Singapore

Nationality British

Rank or Position Sapper. Royal Engineers

> Suddenly one of the officers whipped out his sword, and I thought they had decided to bump me off, but to my amazement he produced a bottle of beer, nipped the top off with his sword, and handed me the bottle. I was then given a loaf of bread. Apart from one or two soldiers, they had treated me very well. My [RAF] wings seemed to fascinate them... No one knows what is going to become of us and everyone tries to guess at our future destination.

'No escape pledge' signed by Ronald Searle in Changi POW camp. In August 1942 the Japanese authorities there required all POWs to sign this undertaking, which was overwhelmingly refused. As a collective punishment, over 15,000 men were herded into the camp's Selarang Barracks area in appalling conditions until their senior officer ordered them to sign. Compliance was deemed invalid as it was done under duress. Many men used false names, most popularly that of Australian outlaw Ned Kelly.

In Singapore, Jack Egan's first thoughts on realising his situation were that 'when Australia needed every man 15,000 of us were idle and useless':

> No doubt you at home felt the same gloom and danger of this period too, but you at least knew what steps were being taken to counter the threat. We pictured only what we knew, namely the victorious Japanese forces, and a vision rose before my mind of Sydney shelled from the sea and bombed from the air, blasted as Singapore had been – Sydney, Townsville, Brisbane, Newcastle, Melbourne and pretty Perth. And after that, landings and more bombing and shelling of smaller places. None escape in war.

Along with most of the British and Australian troops captured in Singapore, Egan was taken to the improvised POW camp complex set up by their captors at Changi, centred on Changi Prison and the adjacent buildings of the former Singapore Garrison. Initially, most of the prisoners' time was spent trying to make the partially destroyed facilities habitable, with little interference by the Japanese. Egan was later sent out into Singapore City on one of many POW work parties, in his case as road-building labour in connection with the construction of memorials at Bukit Batok to the Japanese and Allied dead during the Battle for Singapore. Conditions were largely tolerable, with the POWs experiencing many acts of kindness by local inhabitants:

> In search of food and adventure, men started going outside the wire and passing among the civilians. They were met

> with a friendliness and generosity which passed belief. They were given food to eat and take away. They were given money, barbers shaved them and cut their hair. Those who had been ill were given medicine. Any who wished to stay were given a bed. There was no limit or variety to the extent of the people's kindness, especially the Chinese.

The Japanese guards went along with this for a while, until new and far less tolerant ones replaced them. They included a sadistic individual known to the prisoners as 'the Basher', who frequently subjected them to his unpredictable and violent attentions: 'The man is either a lunatic or a criminal'. In the months and years of captivity to come, POWs all over South-East Asia and the Pacific were to suffer and die at the hands of such Bashers.

POWs were not intended to lead, in Egan's words, 'a blind, useless existence' behind barbed wire. They were to be added to the vast reservoir of slave labour now at Japan's disposal in the territories it had conquered – to be exploited for industrial war production and to help oil the wheels of the Japanese war machine. From their camps, POWs were sent down mines to extract the coal and metals needed for Japan's war effort. They were employed on the construction of airfields and other military infrastructure. They toiled in shipyards to support their captors' naval and mercantile operations. They were sent out to clear the wreckage of war from city streets. Much of it was dangerous work which was performed without basic health and safety measures in place, without adequate food rations, without medical care and with the ever-present likelihood of ill-treatment and arbitrary punishment by the prisoners' taskmasters.

Many thousands were seriously injured or died as a result of workplace accidents and brutal treatment by guards and overseers, frequently compounded by malnutrition and disease. Often the Japanese, perversely, at least buried their POW victims with due respect. Jack Egan was killed in October 1942 in a tree-felling accident and was interred in a Changi cemetery 'with all military honours'. A wreath adorned his grave, with a card in Japanese: 'In the twilight of his life, in the flower of his youth we speed him on his way through the honoured gates.'

Among many Japanese war-related construction projects made possible by POW labour, one in particular, and by far the biggest of them, has come to epitomise the infernal ordeal undergone by so many. The conquest of Burma, and plans for an invasion of India, prompted the Japanese to look for a more secure supply route than was provided by the long and hazardous sea journey around the Malay peninsula to Rangoon. The alternative overland route from Thailand into northern Burma presented a formidable engineering challenge due to mountainous jungle terrain. The British had already considered building a railway in the 1880s but had given up the idea as it was too difficult to carry out. Where Western colonialists had failed, the Japanese were determined to succeed. Construction of the Burma-Thailand Railway began in July 1942 and was completed in October 1943, with the new line running from Ban Pong in Thailand to Thanbyuzayat in Burma, a distance of almost 260 miles. In total, some 61,000 Allied POWs were put to work on the railway, of whom over 12,000 died, half of them from Britain, India and other parts of the Empire. By far the biggest labour contingent was provided by *rōmusha* – Malays, Thais, Burmese, Chinese, Javanese and others – locally conscripted or trafficked from further afield, upwards of 100,000 of them. Their prodigious suffering and deaths went largely unrecorded, the Japanese regarding them as even more expendable than the POWs.

Around 19,000, mainly British and Australian POWs, were taken from Changi and grouped into 6 working parties or Forces. Major Cyril Wild, last encountered at the capitulation of Singapore, was with F Force, comprising 7,000 men and the largest of these work parties. It departed Changi for northern Thailand in April 1943, and most of what was left of it returned to the camp eight months later. Wild was among the survivors and later wrote a 'Narrative of F Force' recording its experiences. It seems that the POWs were told that 'the journey [to Thailand] would entail no marching, and that the force was not required for labour but was destined for "health-camps" in a good climate, where food would be abundant and the unfit would have a better chance of recovery than at Changi'. As Wild's report sets out, the reality was rather different:

Bamboo scaffolding surrounds the bridge under construction at Tamarkan on the Burma-Thailand Railway. This part of the project was immortalised in popular culture in the 1957 blockbuster (and largely fictional) film *The Bridge on the River Kwai*, based on a novel by French writer Pierre Boulle.

> As each party arrived at Bampong [Ban Pong] it learned that the Force was faced with a march of indefinite length as no transport was available. Consequently all the heavy equipment of the Force, including hospital equipment, medical supplies, tools and cooking-gear, and all personal kit which could not be carried on the man, had to be abandoned in an unguarded dump at Bampong...The march of 300 kilometres which followed would have been arduous for fit troops in normal times. For this Force, burdened with its sick and short of food, it proved a trial of unparalleled severity... The march was carried out in stages of 20 to 30 kilometres and lasted two and a half weeks. The parties always marched at night; the monsoon broke in earnest soon after the march began, and conditions rapidly worsened... Men toiled through the pitch blackness and torrential rain, sometimes knee-deep in water, sometimes staggering off bridges in the dark... Of the large and growing number of sick, many fell by the wayside, and they and their kit had to be carried by their comrades.

On arrival at their destination F Force found that their camps had not yet been completed, and they were made to start work immediately with no regard for the hellish forced march they had just survived:

> The work demanded of all men, without consideration of their physical condition, was heavy navvy-labour on the rushed construction of a 50-kilometre stretch of the Burma-Thailand railway, through hilly and flooded jungle, immediately south of the Three Pagodas Pass. This work was arduous in the extreme, men having to carry logs far beyond their strength and pile-drive up to their waists in water. The hours were generally from first light to dark, but frequently men were kept out as late as 2am the following morning. Men working in quarries without boots had their feet badly cut and these cuts developed into tropical ulcers. Through incessant work in deep mud, trench feet became practically universal and rapidly developed into ulcers also. There were daily beatings of officers and men at work, sometimes even into unconsciousness. These beatings were

Ceremonial sleeper spike made to mark the completion of the Burma-Thailand Railway in October 1943. The tracks were built southwards from Burma and northwards from Thailand, meeting at Konkoita (Kaeng Khoi) on the Thai side of the border.

> not for disciplinary purposes but were intended to urge sick and enfeebled men to physical efforts quite beyond their remaining strength, or to punish officers who intervened on their behalf...
>
> By the end of July [1943] the position of the Force was desperate. Communication between the camps and either Burma or Thailand had ceased owing to impassable roads and broken bridges; 1,800 of the Force had died. In one camp alone the following diseases were prevalent: cholera, typhus, spinal meningitis, smallpox, diphtheria, jaundice, pneumonia, pleurisy, malaria, dysentery, scabies, beriberi and tropical ulcers. With the exception of quinine, there were very few drugs and no dressings available throughout the whole area ... Deaths in one camp alone (Sonkurai) were then averaging 12 a day, and of the original 1,600 British troops who marched into that camp in May, 1,200 were dead before December. By the end of December, when the Force arrived back in Singapore, more than 3,000 men were dead out of the original 7,000 who had set out in April ... Of the 3,000 survivors who returned to Singapore, 95 per cent were heavily infected with malaria.

Nightmarish conditions on the Burma-Thailand Railway would have been even worse without the so-called V Scheme or V Organisation, an almost miraculous clandestine network of British POWs, internees and local civilians, notably the Kanchanaburi-based trader Boonpong Sirivejjabhandu, which succeeded in smuggling at least some desperately needed medicines, money and food into many of the railway camps.

Conditions for the vast majority of other POWs were

P.O.W. WORKING ON THAI-BURMA RAILWAY AT KANU CAMP THAILAND 1943

only relatively less grim. In Hong Kong Donald Hill was taken to the Sham Shui Po camp, previously a British Army barracks:

> The whole camp has been stripped of every useful article by looters, and had also been bombed. All doors, windows, furniture and fittings had been taken, leaving just hulks of buildings. Even in peacetime it was an awful dump, but now it looked like a typhoon had hit it... Several men had been here for days, being captured earlier on. Two Warrant Officers had been tied up with wire, stripped of everything, and left for three days without food or water after having seen several of their comrades bayonetted. We get rice twice a day which tastes foul and does not alleviate our hunger.

In Java Andrew Duncan spent the first months of his captivity in the camp at Tandjong Priok, 'a notorious fever spot'. He and his fellow POWs had to make do with accommodation that was 'in a filthy condition, cockroaches, bedbugs, crickets and rats abounding, the latrines being indescribably filthy'. The camp was presided over by a commandant nicknamed Ratface by the prisoners. In October 1942, Duncan and over 1,000 other POWs were transported by sea to Japan to work in the Ube coalmines. These transports were another aspect of the POW ordeal, mostly in dilapidated merchant ships which came to be known as 'hell ships', with good reason. Prisoners were crammed into the holds with little or no fresh air, water or food, on voyages which often took many

Prisoners of War working on Thai-Burma Railway at Kanu [Konyu] *Camp, Thailand 1943* by John Mennie. Thousands of Allied POWs were also put to work in similar conditions on another railway construction project in Sumatra during 1944–1945, of whom around 700 died.

Attendance record for a POW whose labour was exploited in the Mitsubishi copper and tin mines at Akenobe, Japan. What is now a tourist attraction was a highly dangerous working environment for POWs during the war.

weeks and were at the mercy of violent storms or, increasingly as the war progressed, at risk of being torpedoed by prowling US and British submarines. Sometimes prisoners literally went mad and killed or attempted to kill their fellows or themselves. These floating atrocities bore such alluring names as, in Duncan's case, *Yoshida Maru* and *Singapore Maru*.

In this mass of human suffering, POWs managed to adapt, survive and find reasons for surviving against all odds. Thanks to the Red Cross many of them could communicate, if only infrequently and with long delays, with their families, and receive parcels of food and comforts, if these were not diverted for their own use or left to spoil by the Japanese. What their captors failed to provide was often improvised by the prisoners themselves: treatments for sickness and wounds, artificial limbs, dental services, vitamins and food supplements, items of clothing to replace rotting rags, and many other 'fixes' that made existence more tolerable. Where they could do so POWs formed clubs, discussion groups and 'universities' to keep their minds active. They salvaged or made musical instruments, created theatres, stage sets and costumes to put on entertainments or more serious productions, even in some of the worst Railway camps – these were often attended by bemused Japanese camp officials. Many prisoners scrounged writing materials and kept secret diaries or notebooks, at considerable risk of severe punishment if discovered. Others drew the daily scenes of camp life and the people around them, or the

Engraved aluminium rice tin belonging to Dutch POW Thomas Oostveen, captured in Java in March 1942. Oostveen later gave the tin to a British prisoner, RAF serviceman Norman Cornell, who was in the hospital bed next to his in a POW camp in Japan.

Prosthetic leg made from salvaged materials for a British POW in a camp in Thailand.

often spectacular natural world beyond the wire. POW ingenuity was also employed to build, or smuggle, and conceal clandestine wireless receivers, which brought news from the outside world and of the progress of the war, giving a vital lift to morale. As in all human communities there were also examples of less edifying behaviour: prisoners who ran 'rackets' at the expense of their fellows, who stole precious food or other items from prisoners weaker than themselves, who collaborated with their captors in attempts to save their own skins. Captivity brought out some of the best and the worst in human nature.

Much of what was experienced by Japan's POWs was also inflicted on those interned as civilian nationals of the countries with which it was at war. Internees might not have to hew coal deep underground or build railways, but their lives behind barbed wire or walls were just as vulnerable to malnutrition, disease, ill-treatment and general neglect. Arthur Sleep, whose home in Singapore had been bombed before the February 1942 capitulation, joined 3,000 other internees in Changi Prison. Conditions were primitive to start with, and only got worse:

> Our food deteriorated and soon consisted of rice with a few spoonfuls of tinned meat or tinned sardines in the middle of the day. The morning meal was a gruel of rice and water with a cup of local tea, whilst in the evening we had a rice-pudding, so long as we could buy tinned milk and sugar from funds subscribed from the money brought into prison by the internees. The scale of rations was much inferior to the prison diet prescribed in peacetime… All our applications to be allowed a visit from the local Red Cross representative (Swiss) were flatly refused. We knew that we were in for a grim time and that they were concealing our treatment from the British government.

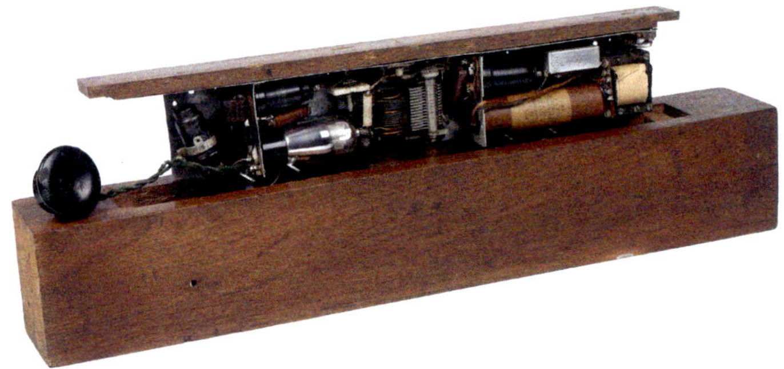

Wireless receiver concealed in the frame of a bunkbed in Changi POW camp. It was operated by two RAF officers, Jeffrey Skinner and Thomas Boyce, who tuned in to British, Indian and Australian radio stations, distributing the news by a carefully controlled word of mouth system. Discovery by the Japanese would have meant severe punishment or death for those involved.

Dickin Medal (the 'animal VC') awarded to English Pointer Judy, the only animal to be officially registered as a POW. A mascot in Royal Navy gunboats on the Yangtze River in China, she was captured along with other crew and stayed with them in captivity in Sumatra. The award citation praised her 'magnificent courage and endurance in Japanese prison camps, which helped to maintain morale among her fellow prisoners and also for saving many lives through her intelligence and watchfulness'.

Judy on board HMS *Grasshopper*.

Conditions in Changi Prison deteriorated even further after October 1943, when internees were collectively punished for an Anglo-Australian commando attack on shipping in Singapore harbour, alongside other acts of sabotage, which the Japanese were wrongly convinced must have been facilitated by 'agents' within the prison. Some internees fell victim to torture and killings by the notorious *Kempeitai*, the Japanese Military Police often likened to the Gestapo in Nazi Germany. This event became known as the Double Tenth Incident, as the searches and arrests happened on 10 October. In May 1944, Sleep and the other Changi Prison internees were relocated to Sime Road camp, which brought little improvement to living conditions or rations:

> The Japanese could have given us better food or allowed us Red Cross supplies or parcels but they deliberately starved us.

In Java another aspect of internment was experienced by Lily Judah. One of 13 children of a Dutch-Jewish family, Lily had set up an eyecare business in Malang with her husband, a qualified optometrist. All was going well, and even after Japan occupied the island in March 1942 Japanese soldiers frequented the shop as paying customers. Lily described subsequent events:

PDSA
For
Gallantry
WE ALSO
SERVE

EPH9321

> The first year started with a strict curfew and the wives of Dutch military men were surrounded and interned. Also, civilian women apart from their husbands. They blocked a whole area of neighbourhood homes and had [the women] live there with barbed wire, surrounded with Japanese guards. We were not intimidated at all. My husband even learned [Japanese] so he could help the sales... Then in early January 1943 there was a hard banging on the door and my husband rushed to open and was approached by stern-looking soldiers with their rifles pointed at him to follow them to a truck waiting outside already full of Jewish men... There was no time to say goodbye, only eye contact. I was less than six months' pregnant.

Lily moved back with her parents, leaving the shop in the care of staff. In August 1943, the rest of the family was also interned. Lily's name was not on the arrest list, but she volunteered to go into internment with her baby daughter so as not to be left behind to further uncertainty:

> Luckily my whole family was assigned one large cell with many others too... Each of us got a small neck pillow and a mat made of banana leaves to sleep on. A tin mug, plate and tin spoon, also a piece of cooked beef and rice, folded in banana leaves for each of us and a barrel of drinking water shared between all of us. The cell was then locked up, leaving us too tired to realise what we went through that day.

To Lily it was clear that for her captors 'the Jews and Freemasons are now the enemies!'. Antisemitism had been an increasing feature of Japanese political and public life since the 1936–1937 Anti-Comintern Pact and the 1940 Tripartite Pact with Nazi Germany and fascist Italy. Although it fell far short of the state-sanctioned anti-Jewish policies in those countries, it manifested itself in measures such as a mass relocation and confinement of Shanghai Jews to the city's ghetto in 1941 where increased restrictions were enforced. Elsewhere, too, Jews like Lily and her family were subjected to discriminatory treatment, at least partly encouraged by notions of a 'Jewish

Peril' (*Yudayaka*). This was one aspect, albeit a distinctive one, of the wider official suspicion of and contempt for all those who were not Japanese.

Like the POWs, many internees also invested considerable effort and creativity in keeping themselves occupied with crafts, entertainments, education and other expressions of their determination to maintain as much of normal life as they could. Margaret Dryburgh, a Presbyterian missionary, was one of many civilians who had managed to escape from Singapore by boat before it fell to the Japanese in 1942. She got as far as Bangka Island off the coast of Sumatra before being captured by the Japanese and interned in the camp at Muntok – 'a pretty little town with attractive buildings, lovely trees and flowers, but the impression it made on us was of horror, apprehension, discomfort and sorrow'. Living conditions, as in most other internment camps, were primitive and overcrowded.

> Even worse than the physical discomfort was the sight of so much wretchedness and pain. Former friends were almost unrecognisable in strange, haphazard garments, with hair soaked in oil from sinking ships, hands raw from clinging to ropes, arms and legs and chins covered with sores, faces drawn by suffering. As the days passed, fresh batches of refugees arrived, some at death's door through exposure and exhaustion... New tales of adventure were circulated: of existence on a waterless beach for days, of concealment in Malay villages where the natives were very kind, of harsh treatment by some in terror of their new conquerors, of the shooting of helpless refugees by the soldiers.

Margaret and others were determined to rise above this misery at Muntok and later in the Palembang camp, principally through communal singing and the formation of a women's Vocal Orchestra:

> Cultural activities sprang up and we arranged discussion groups, language and art classes, travel talks, a choral society and weekly concerts. I thanked God for a good musical memory and was able, on the limited paper available, to write out and harmonise music for a choral work. On Sundays we

Leslie Cole
'45

> gave the use of Garage Nine [a building in the Palembang camp] for morning service and for evening prayers... There was much talent in the camp and by organising musical evenings, choral concerts and services, we were able for a time to forget the barbed wire, our constant hunger and sordid surroundings.

Margaret described many internee deaths and funerals in the diary she managed to keep in captivity, until she herself fell sick and died at Loeboek Linggau in April 1945. She was attended by fellow internee and singer Norah Chambers, in whose opinion she 'should have recovered but, like all the others, was so weak from semi-starvation, that she just couldn't'. Among numerous internee tributes to a remarkable woman was this:

> She was an inspiration to us all. Contact with her meant a real quickening of spiritual, mental and intellectual life. Many would have given up and died, had it not been for her strength of character. The whole camp was unanimous that the concerts and music she arranged were a real uplift. She lost herself in her creative work. She regarded the internment not as so many years wasted, but as an invaluable training ground for learning many priceless lessons.

At the time of Margaret Dryburgh's passing, thousands of internees and POWs had suffered and died under the Japanese yoke, and many more would do so before the war against Japan ended. Although to most it still seemed a distant enough prospect in the spring of 1945, that end was rapidly approaching.

PREVIOUS PAGE *British Women and Children interned in a Japanese Prison Camp, Sime Road, Singapore* (1945) by Leslie Cole

'Badge of Merit' awarded to Vilma Stubbs in Sime Road camp, Singapore, by fellow internee Freddy Bloom, who with others organised a camp school so that children like Vilma could continue their education. After the war, Bloom was a pioneering campaigner for the rights of children with hearing loss.

Recipe book made from scraps of fabric and matting by a teenage girl interned in Java as a birthday present for another camp inmate. Food, and the lack of it, was a constant preoccupation with POWs and internees.

SIME ROAD INTERNMENT CAMP
Girl's
Finishing School
VILMA STUBBS
Badge of Merit
CHRISTMAS 1944

RECIPES

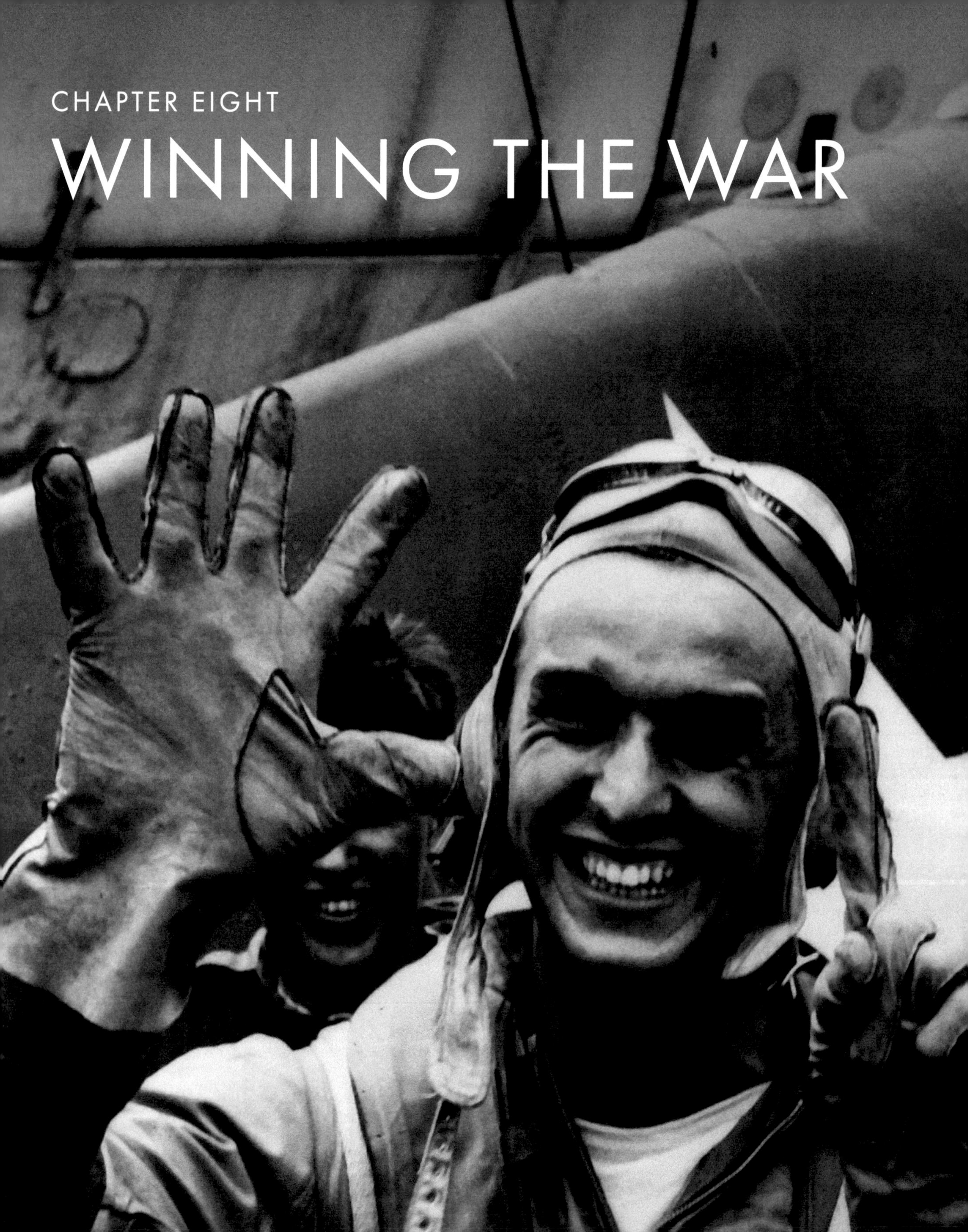

CHAPTER EIGHT

WINNING THE WAR

During the post-war Congressional enquiry into Pearl Harbor, disgraced former US Pacific Fleet commander Admiral Kimmel remarked: 'I never thought those little yellow sons-of-bitches could pull off such an attack, so far from Japan.' Before Japan's large-scale *Blitzkrieg* shattered Western illusions, its soldiers were widely regarded as little more than amusing cartoon characters and no match for white men or troops led by white men. This caricature born of racial prejudice, ignorance and complacency was then replaced by another: the invincible and ubiquitous Asiatic, creating fear and panic. It took many months of fighting actual Japanese soldiers before the Allies began to understand their tactics and ultimately gain the upper hand. The Japanese, too, were obliged to learn much about their adversaries and, more importantly, how fragile the underpinning of their own imperialist hubris was.

The initial successes of Japan's *Blitzkrieg* campaign masked serious domestic issues which, in the long run, contributed significantly to its defeat. Japan, economically and politically, never quite managed to sustain the necessary focus on the demands of total war. Conflict with the West was expected to be relatively short, and the first year or so saw remarkably little economic adjustment to meet war needs. Government planning was characterised by inefficiency and lack of effective control over key industries.

In early 1943, Prime Minister Tōjō took steps to tighten his administration's grip on war-essential production and to rationalise the relevant ministerial structures. This brought some noteworthy improvements, but it did not alter Japan's fundamental economic problem. Ironically, Japan was unable to adequately exploit the raw materials in the countries it had invaded partly for that very purpose, as from 1943 onwards Allied, particularly US submarines, posed too much of a threat to Japanese shipping in those southern waters. Instead, rapidly dwindling domestic stockpiles were plundered and production for civilian consumption steadily curtailed.

US bombers were at the same time increasingly inflicting serious damage on industrial and urban infrastructure, prompting a mass exodus of the civilian population to the countryside and, mostly ineffectual but additionally disruptive, attempts to disperse vital industries away from urban centres.

PREVIOUS PAGE A US Navy Hellcat pilot after shooting down six Japanese aircraft during the Battle of the Philippine Sea, June 1944. The Grumman F6F Hellcat could outperform the Mitsubishi 'Zero' fighter and helped secure US air superiority in the later stages of the Pacific campaign.

On to Japan! (1945) British government poster designed by Severin Rajchman (Sevek). The war in Europe was over, but public opinion had to be primed for the continuation of hostilities in the Asia-Pacific theatre.

ON TO
JAPAN!

Politically the picture was little better. By early 1944, Tōjō was on the face of it a dictator, holding several high civilian and military offices apart from that of prime minister. In reality, his power was severely compromised by that of others – notably his fellow ministers, industrial bosses, court officials and senior military figures. The effective running of both government and economy had always been hampered by persistent rivalry between the army and navy, who competed for influence and resources. As it became clear that Japan itself was under threat of invasion, Tōjō's domestic enemies ganged up against him and forced his resignation in July 1944. His successors could do little to change the overall situation. As the Allies closed in on the home islands, Japan was effectively disintegrating from within.

Britain and the USA, meanwhile, had remained remarkably united with regard to 'grand strategy'. Ever since November 1940, the US armed forces chiefs, known as the Joint Chiefs of Staff from February 1942 onwards, had stuck to the agreed prioritisation of the fight against Nazi Germany and fascist Italy, even if America also found itself at war with Japan. The pivotal naval victory at Midway had confirmed this stance, although at the January 1943 Casablanca Conference it was agreed that enough additional resource should be allocated to the Pacific and South-East Asia to retain the Allied initiative. At the subsequent Quebec Conference in August 1943 a new Allied command structure was decided upon: South East Asia Command (SEAC). Appointed to lead it was Churchill's protegé Admiral Louis Mountbatten, with a US General as

Japanese propaganda matchbox bearing a caricature of Roosevelt being attacked by aircraft, with the slogan 'Certain Victory'.

Three war winners, August 1944: Admiral Sir Bruce Fraser (Commander in Chief of the British Eastern Fleet), Admiral Louis Mountbatten (Supreme Allied Commander SEAC), General Joseph 'Vinegar Joe' Stilwell (commanding US and Nationalist Chinese forces in the China-Burma-India theatre).

Deputy, successively Joseph Stilwell and Raymond Wheeler. Mountbatten's previous job as Chief of Combined Operations highlighted Churchill's enthusiasm for major amphibious operations to retake Burma and Malaya, but these were unrealistic until the planned Normandy landings had happened in North-West Europe and the necessary amphibious capacity freed up.

The immediate beneficiary of the activation of SEAC in November 1943 was the campaign in Burma. Mountbatten made crucial interventions to ensure that Imphal and Kohima were secured in the spring of 1944 and that Mutaguchi's Fifteenth Army was forced into retreat thereafter. In September 1944, Mountbatten was directed to recapture Burma at the earliest date. He proposed two main operations: 'Capital', an advance by Slim's Fourteenth Army towards central Burma, supported by two Chinese armies and complemented by operations in the Arakan towards Akyab and Ramree Island; and 'Dracula', a combined amphibious and airborne assault on Rangoon scheduled for early 1945, before the monsoon season started.

Overall direction of the final campaign in Burma was provided by a newly appointed Commander in Chief Allied Land Forces South-East Asia (ALFSEA, formerly 11th Army Group), Lieutenant General Oliver Leese, fresh from commanding Eighth Army in Italy. Slim was not best pleased at being subordinated to Leese, and, before the Burma campaign ended, the two had an unedifying falling out. Meanwhile, Slim's forces drove 'Capital' at pace and by mid-February 1945 had crossed the Irrawaddy River and were poised to take Mandalay as well as the key communications centre of Meiktila. In a change to the original plan, Slim wrong-footed the Japanese by bringing on the decisive battle in central Burma at Meiktila rather than Mandalay, after which the way to Rangoon was open. On the west coast, Philip Christison's XV Corps secured Ramree Island, which became the main advance air base for the assault on the capital. 'Dracula' was finally carried out, after several postponements, at the beginning of May 1945, when the city was taken by 26th Indian Division, following air landings at Elephant Point by a Gurkha parachute battalion. It took until early August for the remnants of the Japanese Burma Area

Army to be neutralised in a pocket between the Sittang and Salween Rivers north-east of Rangoon, at which point the war in Burma was effectively over.

For Slim, victory in Burma was marred by a messy command quarrel with Leese. Shortly after the capture of Rangoon, the chief of ALFSEA decided to replace Slim with Christison as commander of Fourteenth Army, which was earmarked for the retaking of Malaya. Leese thought Christison, who had more experience of amphibious operations, would do a better job in this role than Slim, who was to be given Twelfth Army to finish the task of clearing the Japanese out of southern Burma. Slim threatened to resign over the loss of his beloved Fourteenth Army, which he had shaped into a formidable fighting force. Leese thereupon sent him home on leave and gave Twelfth Army to Lieutenant General Montagu Stopford instead. In a final almost farcical twist of the tale, Leese was then himself dismissed from command of ALFSEA and replaced by Slim. This was the ultimate vindication of a brilliant leader of men – although Slim had little time to enjoy it before the war ended.

In the Pacific, Nimitz and the US Marine Corps had been pursuing the 'shortest route to Japan' through the Gilbert, Marshall, Caroline and Mariana Islands. By August 1944, the latter were in American hands, after particularly ferocious Japanese resistance on Saipan. Its capture had precipitated the fall of the Tōjō government, and, together with Tinian and Guam, it formed the main base for the forthcoming US bomber offensive against Japan itself. To the west, MacArthur had been tasked with retaking the Philippines. He proposed to land first on the central island of Leyte, using General Walter Krueger's US Sixth Army supported by two naval fleets: Admiral Thomas Kinkaid's 7th and Admiral William 'Bull' Halsey's 3rd. On 20 October 1944, MacArthur fulfilled his promise to return to the Philippines and waded ashore on Leyte – he then did it again for the cameras to make sure the world knew about it.

The Commander in Chief of the Japanese Combined Fleet, Admiral Soemu Toyoda, attempted to disrupt proceedings by luring Kinkaid and Halsey away from Leyte to destroy their fleets in an entrapment operation on an epic scale. A series of smaller but decisive naval engagements between 24–26 October became known collectively as the Battle of Leyte

Gulf and proved to be the Imperial Japanese Navy's last major outing. Damage and loss on both sides was considerable, the Americans only achieving a victory of sorts when the principal Japanese commander, Admiral Takeo Kurita, decided to withdraw from the action for reasons that are still not entirely clear. It was enough to enable the US invasion of the main northern island of Luzon to commence in December 1944, leading to the fall of Manila in March 1945 after some of the fiercest and most destructive urban fighting of the entire war.

In November 1944, the first US heavy bomber raids on the Japanese home islands began from their bases in the Marianas. It was the start of a sustained and devastating assault on Japan's industrial, economic and urban infrastructure, carried out by B-29 Superfortresses of XXI Bomber Command. From January 1945 these were directed by Major General Curtis LeMay, who introduced low-level bombing tactics employing a mix of high explosives and incendiaries. This found its most lethal expression in the March 1945 Operation 'Meetinghouse' raid on Tokyo, in which 25 per cent of the city was destroyed in an apocalyptic firestorm, which by most estimates claimed upwards of 90,000 lives.

Between February and June 1945, US forces took the last two stepping stones to Japan, Iwo Jima and Okinawa. These were crucial breaches of Japan's inner circle of defence and provided more airfields with which to sustain the B-29 offensive. US possession of Okinawa was also a precondition for any Allied invasion of Japan, and in terms of resources committed to it the assault was comparable to the Normandy landings of June 1944. The Japanese defence of Okinawa was predictably fierce, resulting in around 10,000 casualties among Allied naval personnel – Task Force 57 of the British Pacific Fleet helped cover the amphibious landings –and almost 40,000 among the US Marines and infantry troops. Japanese casualties were of a similar order, except with far more dead than wounded.

On the Allied side, a significant proportion of the total casualties was caused by a Japanese innovation that had first been tried out on American ships at Leyte Gulf, which involved the deliberate crashing of Japanese aircraft into Allied ships to cripple or sink them and cause maximum casualties among the

US Marine using a flamethrower against Japanese defences during the Battle for Saipan, June 1944. Almost the entire Japanese garrison of 30,000 troops died in the fighting on this Pacific island, possession of which enabled the Americans to launch their B-29 bomber offensive against Japan.

NORMAN HOWARD

crews. These suicide or *kamikaze* ('divine wind') attacks took a number of forms, including submarines and boats as well as the more common aircraft variant. They were all grouped into so-called Special Attack Units and were a measure of the increasing desperation of Japanese defence efforts. A *kamikaze* aircraft attack was experienced in July 1945 by Peter Booth, a Royal Navy Signalman on board HMS *Sussex* with the Eastern Fleet, covering minesweeping operations off the coast of Thailand. He recorded the event in his diary on 26 July:

> Action Stations all day. Around 1400 hours one of the officers on the compass platform said 'Oh look sir, three of our aircraft returning from a strike'. Just as he said it the aircraft coming over the headland swooped down to sea-level and came straight at the ship and me standing on the starboard side of the bridge! The Captain shouted, 'They are not ours, they are Jap suicide planes – OPEN FIRE!' All hell let loose as every gun on the starboard side opened up – one plane was shot down immediately – a second hit the water immediately in front of the No 2 starboard 4-inch AA guns and ricocheted into the side of the ship – the third

PREVIOUS PAGE *The Battle of the Leyte Gulf* by Norman Howard (undated).

Aftermath of a *kamikaze* attack on USS *Bunker Hill* at Okinawa, May 1945. Some 400 US servicemen were killed – Fred Draeger was among the survivors.

'Lucky charm' worn by US Navy Aviation Ordnanceman Fred Draeger during his service in the aircraft carrier USS *Bunker Hill*.

was blown up into the air by the sheer weight of the gunfire straight over the bridge – I looked up and saw the 'rising sun' markings on its wings, and then it plunged down onto a fleet minesweeper HMS *Vestal* – poor devils, there was an explosion and within minutes it was ablaze. When the Jap flew directly over me on the starboard side of the bridge I thought 'This is too hot for me' and ducked round to the port side just in time to see it hit the *Vestal*.

Twenty of *Vestal*'s crew were killed in the attack and the stricken ship was deliberately sunk by gunfire from a Royal Navy destroyer. She is reported to have been the last Royal Navy ship to be sunk during the war.

Elsewhere in the world other significant events were happening. US President Roosevelt died on 12 April 1945, two months after attending the major Allied conference at Yalta. His main concern at that time was to secure Soviet entry into the war against Japan as soon as possible after the imminent defeat of Nazi Germany. In a manoeuvre entirely worthy of the wily Soviet leader, Roosevelt and Stalin made a secret agreement at Yalta in which the US President secured this objective in return for territorial concessions and guarantees in Mongolia, South Sakhalin and the Kurile Islands. Churchill and Chiang Kai-shek were not informed, even though the agreement partly affected China's own interests. Roosevelt was succeeded in April 1945 by his former vice-president Harry Truman, to whom it fell to bring what Roosevelt had initiated at Yalta to a successful conclusion.

In May 1945, the war in Europe finally came to an end. Following Germany's unconditional surrender across two days on 7 and 8 May, the latter date was officially celebrated as VE – 'Victory in Europe' – Day. While millions of people there and across the world rejoiced at the defeat of Hitler and his Nazi regime, for millions more the war continued. To many of those still fighting and dying in South-East Asia and the Pacific, VE Day seemed remote and irrelevant to their own immediate experiences. Many British soldiers who had fought their way into Germany with the British Liberation Army now joked grimly that BLA stood for 'Burma Looms Ahead', as the prospect of being transferred there dramatically increased.

Captured Japanese suicide boat (*shinyo*) and crew in Hong Kong. These motorboats carried an explosive charge to be detonated on impact with Allied shipping and were also equipped with anti-ship rockets. Operational successes were few compared with *kamikaze* aircraft.

A photograph captioned 'Human anti-tank mines in Burma' shows a Japanese soldier shot dead by British troops before he could activate the bomb he still clutches.

In Britain itself, a political sea-change occurred in the General Election of July 1945, when Churchill was turned out of office in favour of Labour leader Clement Attlee, who had been Churchill's Deputy Prime Minister in the wartime coalition government. Churchill had led the country through the war, but now its people were looking to a better post-war future. Margaret Dryburgh, interned in far-off Sumatra, articulated something of the popular mood which drove the Labour landslide, although she did not live to hear of it:

> Yes, Muntok spelt misery. Yet in the horrors there were flashes of light – self-sacrificing service, a new sense of values, a determination to try one day to share in repairing weaknesses in our social and political structure so ruthlessly exposed by the war.

Peter Booth, trying to avoid being killed by suicide aircraft in the Andaman Sea, wrote in his diary:

> News from home that an election held whilst the war is still on resulted in the Labour Party winning – Clem Attlee replacing Churchill as our leader – although at 19 I am too young to vote it's a shock. Obviously the people at home think the war is over since Hitler was beaten – they should come out here or the Pacific.

The change from Churchill to Attlee came midway through the last major Allied wartime conference, at Potsdam during July–August 1945. On 26 July, the leaders of the USA, Great Britain and China issued the Potsdam Declaration setting out the terms of surrender for Japan, with whom the USSR was not yet at war. They specified a period of Allied occupation, the punishment of war criminals, moves towards a more democratic system of government, and a restructure of the economy to prevent future rearmament or foreign conquests. No mention was made of the Emperor, although the Declaration stated more generally that 'the authority and influence of those who have deceived and misled the people of Japan into embarking on world conquest must be eliminated for all time.' It was not clear if this implied and included the removal of Hirohito and the end of the Imperial House of Japan, as the ultimate authority which had sanctioned the country's expansionist aggression. For Japan's civilian and military leaders this was an unthinkable prospect, and the Allies' subsequent refusal to guarantee the Emperor's position was a major stumbling block to an acceptance of surrender terms.

Not at all ambiguous was the Allied call for an immediate and unconditional surrender of Japan's armed forces: 'The alternative for Japan is prompt and utter destruction.' Except that Allied – mainly American – military planning for ending the war, codenamed 'Downfall', envisaged a long and costly invasion of the Japanese home islands against fanatical resistance. In view of this, the reference to 'prompt and utter destruction' has been widely seen as a veiled pointer to a new weapon which had been tested in the desert of New Mexico on 16 July 1945, ten days before the Declaration was issued.

The idea of a 'super-weapon' using atomic fission had been floated as early as 1904, but it was not until the Second World War that the science and technology progressed far enough to make it a reality. American, British and Canadian expertise was drawn together under the aegis of the US-led Manhattan Project, following Roosevelt's authorisation of the development of the atom bomb in January 1942. It was driven initially by fears that German nuclear scientists would build such a weapon before the Allies could catch up, but its potential use against Japan was an increasingly important factor as the war progressed. As soon as the finished product was successfully tested at Alamogordo on that fateful 16 July, Truman knew that he now held the trump card, not just against Japan but also against an increasingly fractious and unpredictable Soviet Union.

In Tokyo the Potsdam Declaration got a mixed reception. Emperor Hirohito strongly favoured acceptance. Although he had initially given the war his blessing, for most of it he had been urging Tōjō and his ministers to end it as soon as possible, either by a 'decisive battle' or by negotiation. Military leaders were determined to continue the fight, no matter what. A peace party of sorts did exist among former ministers, diplomats and members of the imperial family, and there were some

ENOLA
GAY
NO

diplomatic efforts to persuade the USSR to broker a peace deal with the Western Allies. But the military hawks held sway. Japan's last wartime Prime Minister, Admiral Kantarō Suzuki, prevaricated and failed to give the Allies the assurances they were demanding. Truman decided that it was time to give Japan a taste of what 'prompt and utter destruction' could look like.

In the early hours of 6 August 1945, the B-29 *Enola Gay*, piloted by Colonel Paul Tibbets, lumbered off the airstrip at North Field on Tinian, carrying the 9,700 lb weight of a nuclear device nicknamed 'Little Boy'. It arrived over the city of Hiroshima, which had until then received relatively little attention from LeMay's B-29s and was considered a promising target in other respects, in company with two other aircraft carrying scientific and photographic equipment. At 08.15 the bomb was released. Tibbets had difficulty controlling *Enola Gay* as she suddenly lost weight, and struggled again as the shock waves from the explosion hit his aircraft almost ten miles away from the blast's epicentre. Awed by the brilliant flash and the subsequent monstrous mushroom-shaped cloud boiling upwards, a crew member reportedly exclaimed 'My God, what have we done?' Among those on the ground who witnessed what had been done was a German Jesuit priest and university lecturer, Father Johannes (John) Siemes, who was just outside the city and later wrote an account for American investigators:

> I am sitting in my room at the Novitiate of the Society of Jesus in Nagatsuka... Suddenly (the time approximately 08.14) the whole valley is filled by a garish light which resembles the magnesium light used in photography, and I am conscious of a wave of heat. I jumped to the window to find out the cause of this remarkable phenomenon, but I see nothing more than the brilliant light... On my way from the window I hear a moderately loud explosion which seems to come from a distance, and at the same time the windows are broken with a loud crash. There has been an interval of perhaps 10 seconds since the flash of light... I realise now that a bomb has burst and I am under the impression that it exploded directly over our house or in the immediate vicinity... Most of my colleagues have been injured by fragments of glass.

Colonel Paul Tibbets beside his B-29 *Enola Gay* which delivered the first operational nuclear weapon to its target over Hiroshima on 6 August 1945. He named the aircraft after his mother.

Having tended to their own wounded, Siemes and fellow priests then went out into the city to help others:

> Where the city stood, everything as far as the eye can reach is a waste of ashes and ruins. Only several skeletons of buildings, completely burned out in the interior, remain. The banks of the river are covered with dead and wounded, and the rising waters have here and there covered some of the corpses. On the broad streets in the Hakushima district, naked, burned cadavers are particularly numerous. Among them are the wounded who still live. A few have crawled under burned-out autos and trams. Frightfully injured forms beckoned to us and collapsed. An old woman with a girl whom she was pulling along with her falls at our feet. We place them on our cart and wheel them to the hospital, at whose entrance a dressing station has been set up... We convey another soldier and an old woman to this place, but we cannot move everybody who lies exposed in the sun. It would be hopeless and it is questionable whether those whom we drag to the dressing station come out alive, because even here, nothing effective can be done.

Japan's leaders continued to argue about war or peace. On 9 August another B-29, *Bockscar*, piloted by Major Charles Sweeney, who had flown one of the accompanying aircraft over Hiroshima, headed out from Tinian bearing a second nuclear device, 'Fat Man'. His primary target was the city of Kokura, with Nagasaki the secondary target if weather conditions over the first were unfavourable. They were, so at just after 11am 'Fat Man' exploded over Nagasaki, with equally devastating consequences for that city. Exact figures were and are impossible to determine, but it is likely that up to 240,000 people died in both cities either immediately or within days of the atomic explosions. Many more died later – often many years later – from the effects of exposure to radiation. Among the casualties were Allied POWs who until then had survived in nearby camps.

That same day another event occurred which for most of the leadership in Tokyo, particularly among the military, was of even more consequence than the dropping of atomic bombs.

PREVIOUS PAGE Hiroshima after the bomb. Most buildings were destroyed or severely damaged by the initial blast, the subsequent firestorm consumed everything flammable.

Boeing B-29 bomber on its way to Tokyo, December 1944. The original caption reads: 'This is the first photograph of a Superfortress over Japan, which Saipan-based B-29s are striking with increasing frequency and severity.'

DAILY NEWS

Copr. 1945 by News Syndicate Co. Inc. NEW YORK'S PICTURE NEWSPAPER Trade Mark Reg. U. S. Pat. Off.

Vol. 27. No. 38 — New York, Wednesday, August 8, 1945★ — 52 Main + 4 Manhattan Pages — 2 Cents IN CITY LIMITS | 3 CENTS Elsewhere

ATOM BOMB HIT-A CITY VANISHED

Jap Seaport Went Up in Smoke And Flame, Witnesses Say

40,000-FT. DUST PYRE OVER HIROSHIMA

Story on Page 3.

Stalin finally made good on his promise to enter the war against Japan, and early on 9 August a massive force commanded by Marshal Aleksandr Vasilevsky crossed the border into Manchuria. The Japanese Kwantung Army under General Otozō Yamada was heavily outnumbered and outmanoeuvred, and Soviet forces quickly looked set to roll right across Manchuria and into Korea. Hardliners in Tokyo were even then unable to bring themselves to accept the inevitable, and Prime Minister Suzuki took the unprecedented step of asking the Emperor to personally decide the issue. On 10 August Hirohito decreed an acceptance of the Allied terms and on 14 August recorded a message to that effect to be broadcast to the Japanese people the following day. A group of desperados plotted a coup to prevent Hirohito's message from being aired, but it failed when the audio discs could not be found and seized in time. Many of those involved committed suicide rather than endure the shame of defeat, as did numerous others in the days to come. Japan had finally run out of road, and its war was at an end.

PREVIOUS PAGE The distinctive 'mushroom cloud' rises above Nagasaki after the detonation of the second atomic bomb, 9 August 1945.

PREVIOUS PAGE Front page of the New York *Daily News* two days after Hiroshima.

Soviet troops pose in front of the railway station in Harbin following the Red Army's rapid conquest of Japanese-occupied Manchuria in August 1945.

濱爾哈
ХАРБИН

CHAPTER NINE

VJ DAY AND AFTER

PREVIOUS PAGE Douglas MacArthur signs the Japanese surrender document on the deck of USS *Missouri*, 2 September 1945. Directly behind him stand Generals Jonathan Wainwright and Arthur Percival, looking gaunt after three years in Japanese POW camps.

Japanese officers surrender their swords in Kuala Lumpur, Malaya, in September 1945.

At midday on 15 August 1945 (Japan Standard Time) Hirohito's message to 'Our good and loyal subjects' was broadcast. For most of those listening to this Imperial Rescript on the Termination of the War, it was the first time they had ever heard the voice of their Emperor. In what to Western ears was an excruciatingly formal, monotonous and strangely chant-like speech, Hirohito informed his people that 'after pondering deeply the general trends of the world and the actual conditions obtaining in Our Empire today, We have decided to effect a settlement of the present situation by resorting to an extraordinary measure. We have ordered Our Government to communicate to the Governments of the United States, Great Britain, China and the Soviet Union that Our Empire accepts the provisions of their Joint Declaration [at Potsdam].' After a review of the reasons for this decision, Hirohito concluded his speech with an exhortation to the people of Japan to unite their strength 'to be devoted to the construction of the future. Cultivate the ways of rectitude; foster nobility of spirit; and work with resolution so as you may enhance the innate glory of the Imperial State and keep pace with the progress of the world'.

President Truman had been advised of the surrender decision earlier that day, and due to the Tokyo – Washington DC time difference was able to announce it in the early evening of 14 August. He declared that the proclamation of VJ – 'Victory over Japan' – Day 'must wait upon the formal signing of the surrender terms by Japan'. This took place on 2 September 1945, aboard the battleship USS *Missouri* anchored in Tokyo Bay. Douglas MacArthur was the principal signatory of the Instrument of Surrender on behalf of the Allied nations, while for Japan the signatories were Foreign Minister Mamoru Shigemitsu and Chief of the Army General Staff Yoshijirō Umezu. While this date officially marked VJ Day in the USA, elsewhere it was widely associated at the time and since with the date(s) of the announcements by Truman and Hirohito, when the first public celebrations began. These were experienced in London by Noelle Williams, serving with an anti-aircraft regiment as a member of the Auxiliary Territorial Service (ATS):

14th August ...11.50 [pm]: I am woken up by Gordon knocking on my door saying the Prime Minister is going to broadcast in 10 minutes. This surely must be the news we have been waiting for so many days and I am told to get up and go to the mess for a drink ... The minutes seem long and at last Clement Attlee comes to the microphone to say that Japan has surrendered. Wild excitement and we cheer lustily. After a short thanksgiving service on the wireless we make as much noise as we can, wake up the camp and open the wet bar – free beer all round and this soon gets the gunners and ATS out of bed!

Japanese soldier's personal flag (*yosegaki hinomaru*) with messages from family, friends and acquaintances of its owner, Ken'ichirō Kameuchi, retrieved from the Imphal battlefields by Private William Palmer of The Devonshire Regiment and taken home as a war souvenir.

She later joined the VJ Day revellers in central London:

Going down Oxford Street I ran into a paperstorm – torn up telephone directories being dropped from the rooftops onto the crowds below... I certainly hadn't bargained for the crowds. Rainbow Corner [an American Red Cross club off Piccadilly Circus] was simply terrific... The Americans from the Rainbow Club were on the balcony with a band and we all sang lustily. 'Tipperary' again made me weep a bit – silly but I just couldn't help it. It is our proudest hour and anything patriotic always makes me feel emotional... Trafalgar Square has a band playing and plenty of loudspeakers... Quite a stir is caused by some sailors who have 'borrowed' a road sweepers' cart and broom and are riding madly round strewing the refuse in front of them as if it were rose leaves!

Elsewhere, celebrations were more low-key. Aboard HMS *Sussex* off Ceylon (Sri Lanka), Peter Booth was marking his birthday:

Although I was too young to receive the grog (rum) ration, everybody in the mess and the Yeoman gave me sippers which made me quite squiffy – then, at 1600 hours we heard the Japs had surrendered following the dropping of the second Atomic Bomb – Good-oh! After we had anchored just outside Trincomalee harbour boom the Skipper ordered 'Splice the mainbrace', an additional rum issue and, yes, because it was my birthday – again sippers all round – Magic!

– it's VJ Day… and we let off fireworks again and searchlights, just like VE Day in Malta.

Sussex then proceeded to Singapore where she hosted the local surrender of Japanese forces on 5 September. Arthur Sleep, in the Sime Road internment camp, described what happened there:

> The termination of our captivity under the Japanese was marked by the hoisting of the Union Jack in camp by Lady Thomas, wife of our former Governor [Sir Shenton Thomas], who had been with us during internment and had shown great fortitude. Our own internees' band played the National Anthem as the flag unfurled in the morning breeze. This was the moment we had been waiting for. It was too intense for

> most of the internees to sing the verses, but when it came to 'Land of Hope and Glory' we found our voices and the echoes must have been heard by wondering and apprehensive Japanese on the road to Singapore.

Over 100,000 POWs and internees across a vast area now had to be located, provided with information on what was happening and what to do next, supplied with food and other essentials, given medical aid, and prepared for their return home. Millions of leaflets and emergency supplies were air-dropped by the Allies (Operations 'Birdcage' and 'Mastiff'), and thousands of those POWs in most need of medical attention were loaded onto the return flights. Much of the initial work on the ground was done by specialist teams of the Recovery of Allied Prisoners of War and Internees (RAPWI) organisation under the auspices of Mountbatten's South East Asia Command. The plight of those liberated from camps and prisons was witnessed by many, including Peter Booth during HMS *Sussex*'s sojourn in Singapore:

> Prisoners of War are being released from Changi Camp, medically checked and some of them being brought down to the *Sussex* which is now open house to entertain and feed them – poor devils. People ashore are starving so the galley are sending hundreds of loaves ashore. I helped POWs down the gangway to our messdeck literally having to lift their feet up one by one – they are like skeletons – so thin their feet slip out of the boots issued to them… It was heartbreaking to see the poor devils and couldn't do enough for them, a number of us wrote letters home for some of them that hadn't the strength to write – we listened to their tales of treatment – the Japs were animals!… When they were due to return to hospital camp we had to carry most of them up to the deck – they were so thin and light weight not many of them could manage to walk up.

Administering the care and repatriation of such large numbers was a complex and lengthy process, but most were back on home soil by the end of 1945. There was inevitably some impatience with delays in getting there, RAPWI being renamed 'Retain All Prisoners of War Indefinitely' by many disgruntled men. The repatriation journeys could take many weeks, those to the UK often going via North America, but this was also part of the recuperation process. When they did finally arrive home most former POWs, and many former internees, found that their ordeal was by no means over. Physical and mental scars persisted, often until the end of lives cut short by what they had suffered. Longterm ill-health caused by the circumstances of captivity was a major issue. Large numbers of repatriated POWs disembarked at Liverpool, and many of these were helped in the months and years to come by the expertise of specialists at the Liverpool School of Tropical Medicine. Others received similar care at Queen Mary's Hospital, Roehampton, in London. But many suffered in silence, neither seeking nor being offered the help they needed.

The Royal message of 'welcome home' given to returning British POWs expressed the hope 'that your return from captivity will bring you and your families a full measure of happiness, which you may long enjoy together'. All too often this remained a pious wish. Official help for ex-POWs was minimal to non-existent. Many were told not to speak to the press about their experiences and were discouraged even from discussing details with family members. Donald Hill, who had survived the Battle of Hong Kong and long years of captivity, was one of the many who rarely, if ever, talked about what had happened to them. He had written his wartime diary in a seemingly impenetrable numerical code, disguised as 'mathematical tables' to avoid Japanese scrutiny, which was finally deciphered many years after his death in 1985. Only then, in the twilight of her own life, was his widow able to understand what he had endured during the war and what had tormented him ever since.

Allied POWs and internees figured largely, but by no means exclusively, in the grim catalogue of atrocities carried out by Japanese military and civilian personnel during many years of war. Planning for the prosecution of war crimes and crimes against humanity had begun in 1943, and at Potsdam in July 1945 the Allies had declared that 'stern justice shall be meted out to all war criminals, including those who have visited cruelties upon our prisoners'. Representatives of

Singapore: Limbless Officers and Men Checking Out from Changi Gaol by Leslie Cole (1946).

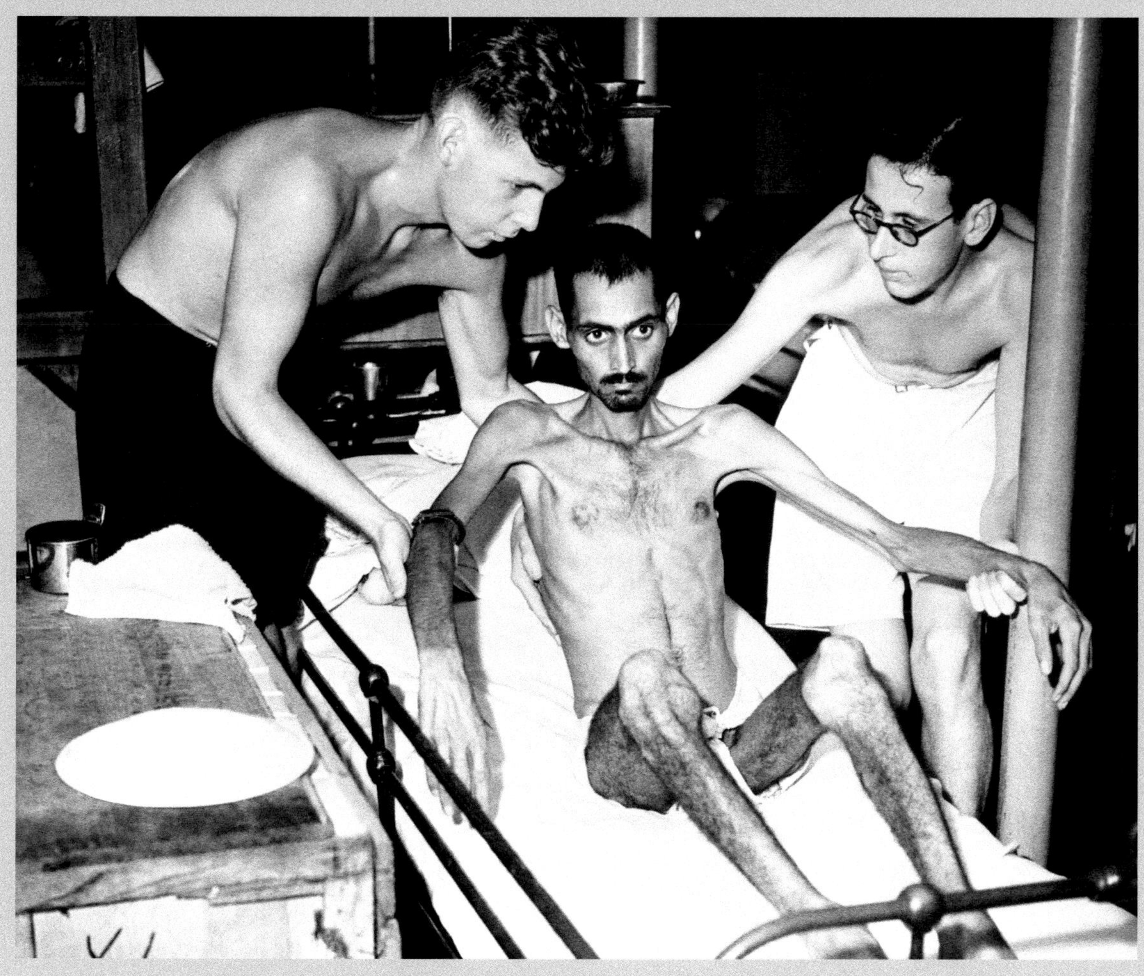

A liberated Indian POW in Hong Kong receiving medical attention on board the hospital ship HMHS *Oxfordshire*.

Japan's wartime leadership were tried by the International Military Tribunal for the Far East in Tokyo from April 1946 to November 1948. Chief among the defendants was Hideki Tōjō, who was sentenced to death and dispatched by the hangman shortly after the trial ended. Among the many prosecution witnesses called to give their testimony in the courtroom was Vivian Bullwinkel, one of a group of Australian Army nurses who had escaped from Singapore in the ship *Vyner Brooke* in February 1942, only to fall into the hands of Japanese soldiers on Bangka Island off the coast of Sumatra. Many of the passengers and crew had already been killed by the soldiers before these returned to the beach where 22 nurses and a civilian had remained:

> When [the soldiers] had finished cleaning their rifles and bayonets, then they ordered the twenty-three of us to march into the sea. We had gone a few yards into the water when they commenced to machine-gun from behind. I saw the girls fall one after the other, when I was hit. The bullet that hit me struck me in the back at about waist level and passed straight through. It knocked me over, and the waves brought me in to the edge of the water. I continued to lie there for ten or fifteen minutes, and then I sat up and looked around, and the Japanese party had disappeared. I then took myself up into the jungle and became unconscious.

Vivian was one of only three survivors of the massacre, in which all of her colleagues died. Apart from the high-level Tokyo tribunal, numerous regional trials were held by the Allied nations to process the majority of those deemed responsible for committing war crimes 'on the ground'. Conspicuously absent from any courtroom, and never formally called to account for his role in Japan's wars of aggression, was Emperor Hirohito. Despite widespread Allied expectations and demands for Hirohito to stand public trial, Douglas MacArthur in his capacity as Supreme Commander for the Allied Powers of occupation in Japan (SCAP) had other ideas. He intended to use the Emperor's residual authority and continued popular veneration in Japan to help progress democratic reforms and the establishment of a more constitutional type of monarchy.

Former Prime Minister Tōjō after a failed suicide attempt to avoid Allied custody and trial, September 1945.

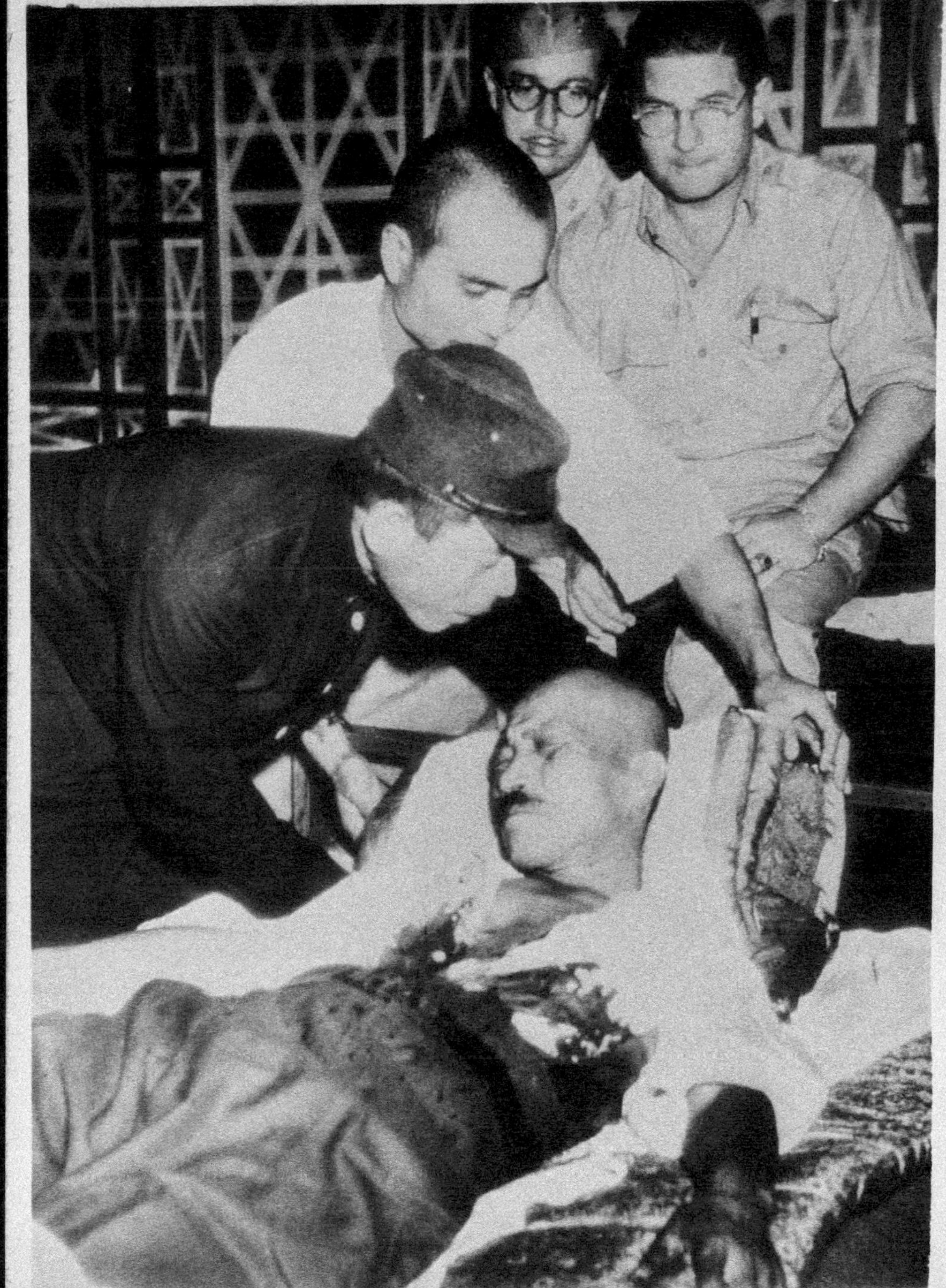

Hirohito was happy to oblige. In any case MacArthur had plenty of axes to grind with others, among them General Yamashita, the 'Tiger of Malaya' who in the last stages of the war had been tasked with attempting to prevent the Americans retaking the Philippines, MacArthur's home turf. He was tried and held responsible for many atrocities which took place there, with his name also being associated with war crimes committed under his overall command in Malaya and Singapore –notably the massacre of patients and staff at the Alexandra Military Hospital. His death sentence was nonetheless controversial, but MacArthur refused to consider his appeal and Yamashita went to the gallows.

Brought in with Japanese POWs in Burma, these Chinese were among the vast number of so-called 'comfort women' subjected to sexual exploitation and abuse in Japanese army brothels during the war.

CHAPTER TEN

END OF EMPIRES

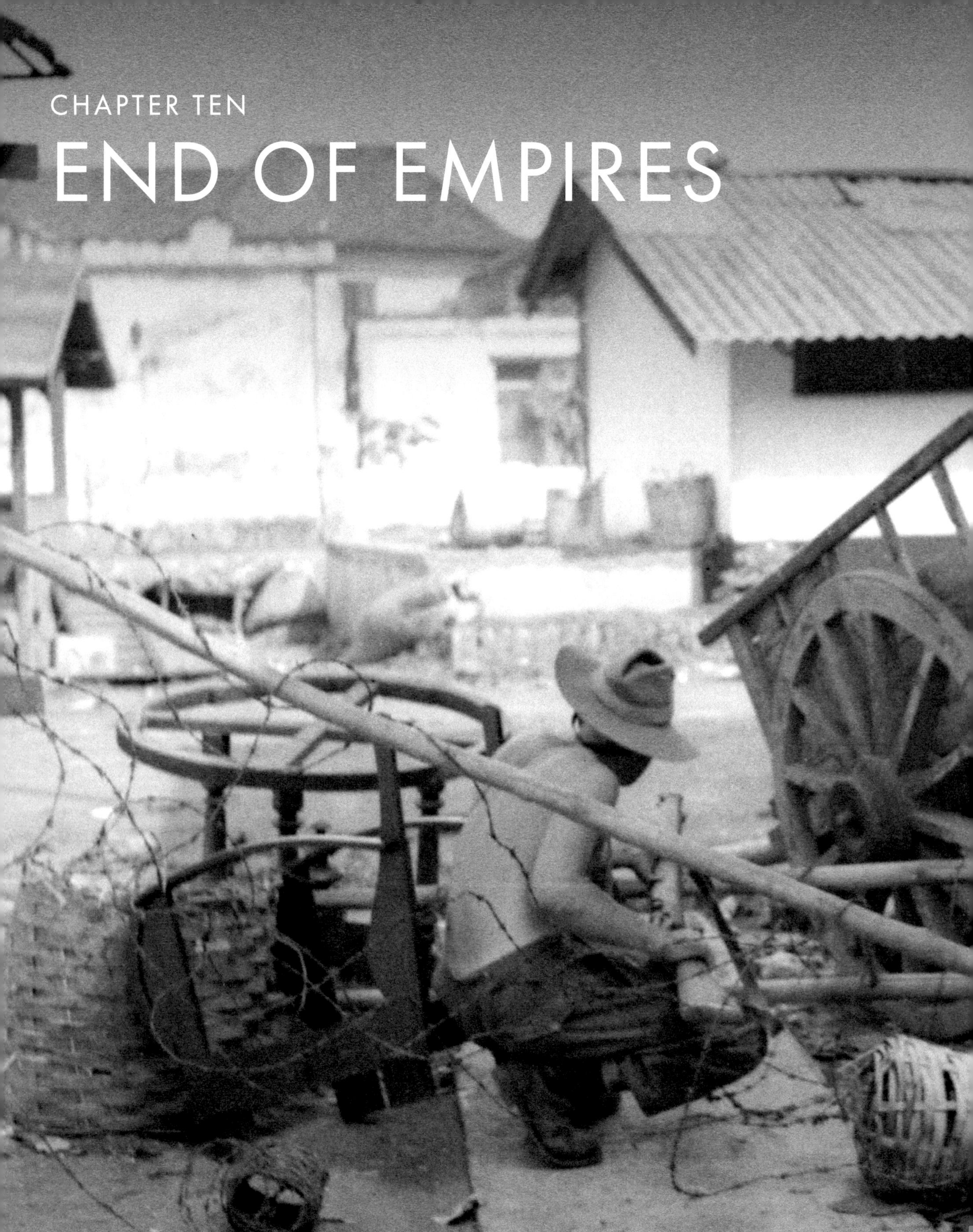

Douglas MacArthur presided over the occupation, demilitarisation and democratisation of Japan from 1945 to 1952, which involved an Allied military presence to the tune of almost a million servicemen, including 40,000 British Commonwealth Occupation Force troops. It was the beginning of a significant transformation of Japanese political and social structures in the aftermath of defeat. But it was not simply a matter of the victors imposing change on the vanquished. Across South-East Asia the war acted as a catalyst for and accelerator of similarly profound changes, particularly with regard to the longstanding colonial interests of the Allied powers themselves. The United Nations Charter of October 1945 referred to those territories 'whose peoples have not yet attained a full measure of self-government', requiring the administering powers 'to develop self-government, to take due account of the political aspirations of the peoples, and to assist them in the progressive development of their free political institutions'. As always, reality rarely conformed to elegant rhetoric.

The end of the Dutch East Indies was notably messy and violent. Indonesian nationalists led by Achmed Sukarno declared independence shortly after VJ Day in mid-August 1945. Sukarno had received Japanese backing during the war in an attempt to harness popular support for Tokyo's occupation policies and war effort. The Dutch authorities were determined to reassert their colonial control, which they succeeded in doing with British help. Peter Booth was one of many British and Indian servicemen whose demobilisation was delayed by their being sent to Java to 'quell the uprising of terrorists' – a misnomer he partly corrected to 'Indonesian rebels' elsewhere in his diary. However, the tide of history could not be stemmed indefinitely and Sukarno became the first President of the Republic of Indonesia in 1949.

During his tenure as wartime leader, Churchill had made no secret of the fact that as far as he was concerned one of Britain's main war objectives was to recover those imperial possessions which the Japanese had taken. As he declared in 1942, 'I have not become the King's First Minister in order to preside over the liquidation of the British Empire.' Attlee took a more progressive view, but this did not stop Britain moving swiftly

PREVIOUS PAGE British soldiers take cover behind an improvised barricade in Surabaya, Java, during operations against Indonesian nationalists in 1945.

Indian National Army propaganda poster issued at the time of the Imphal-Kohima offensive in 1944, featuring the image and words of Subhas Chandra Bose: 'The Provisional Government of Azad Hind will fight until the British and American forces are either crushed or are driven out of India... Who could check this fierce fire of Independence?'

JAI HIND! HAMARE BHAYIYO! BAHADURISE HATH ME HATHIAR LEKAR HAM UTTH KHARE HUE HAIN
AZAD HIND KA QAUMI JHANDA SARHAD KO PAR KAR HAMARI MATRI-BHUMI KI ZAMIN PAR FAHARAH RAHA HAI
Sisters and Brothers! The Indian National Army under the command of the Provisional Government of Azad Hind, which was established at Shonan on Octover 21, 1943, in accordance with the general will of the 3-million Indians in East Asia, has advanced deep into India after crossing the national border.
The provisional Government of Azad Hind, which is your government, aims at realizing only one mission... the establishment of a permanent National Government of Free India based upon the will of the Indian people by driving out British and American troops from the sacred soil of India.
The Provisional Government of Azad Hind will fight until the British and American forces are either crushed or are driven out of India.
Simultaneously, the Government will advance toward the construction of the liberated areas...
Sisters and Brothers! Today when the enemy is being driven out of India, you have returned to yourselves, in other words, you have returned to the nation of freedom!
COME AND JOIN THE PROVISIONAL GOVERNMENT OF AZAD HIND WHICH IS YOUR OWN GOVERNMENT! ASSIST THE DEFENCE OF FREE INDIA WHICH YOU HAVE NEWLY ACQUIRED!
SUBHAS CHANDRA BOSE
Highest Commander of the Indian National Army

Indian National Army cap badge, bearing the INA motto 'Unity, Faith and Sacrifice'.

to reoccupy Hong Kong in August and September 1945, partly to avoid a potential transfer of the territory to Chinese control – an event Britain managed to avert for the next 52 years, until Hong Kong became a 'special administrative region' of the People's Republic in 1997.

Britain tried to retain and simplify its control over Malaya by creating the Malayan Union in 1946, with Singapore remaining a separate Crown colony. These plans were crossed by the Malayan Communist Party, which had received British support against the Japanese occupiers during the war in its manifestation as the Malayan People's Anti-Japanese Army (MPAJA). The communists spearheaded an insurgency against British rule between 1948 and 1960, the so-called Malayan Emergency, leading to many years of conflict and unrest even after the 1957 Malayan Declaration of Independence. Singapore, too, suffered a long period of political, social and economic disruption from 1945 onwards, strongly influenced by events in Malaya, until it finally achieved independence as a republic in 1965.

In Burma the war had been fought to a significant extent by the country's inhabitants, with Burmese, Chins, Kachins, Nagas, Karens (like Neville Hogan) and others fighting alongside the British, Indian and African forces there or helping them in other capacities. The Japanese on the other hand exploited anti-British sentiment in various ways, notably by assisting in the creation of the Burma Independence Army (BIA) in December 1941 under the leadership of Aung San. Many BIA soldiers accompanied the Japanese in their invasion and occupation of Burma, and after the conquerors proclaimed Burma's 'independence' in August 1943, many thousands more were recruited into the renamed Burma National Army. In April 1945 Aung San and the BNA defected to the British, which helped to smooth the way towards Burma's actual independence in January 1948 – although Aung San, who played a key role in this process, was assassinated on the orders of his political rival and former Prime Minister U Saw.

In India, wartime events also had a crucial impact on the country's fortunes after 1945. The end of British rule in India had been on the cards for many years. In 1942 the subject was brought into sharp focus by Churchill's dispatch of senior

British government minister Sir Stafford Cripps to Delhi to negotiate full Indian buy-in to the war effort in exchange for the promise of future self-government with Dominion status. Cripps's proposals were widely seen as delaying tactics and failed to persuade the Indian National Congress. They were also rejected by Muslim League leader Muhammad Ali Jinnah, and contributed to the launching of the Quit India Movement by Mohandas (Mahatma) Gandhi later the same year. This resulted in mass arrests and repression by the British authorities, achieving the very opposite of the Cripps Mission's aims. Japan, in contrast, seemed to have more success in harnessing popular anti-British and pro-independence opinion to its own agenda. A branch of the Indian Independence League (IIL) had existed in Tokyo since 1937 and during the Malayan campaign the IIL leadership in Thailand collaborated with the Japanese Army in recruiting disaffected Indian troops into the League. After the fall of Singapore in February 1942, an Indian National Army (INA) was formed by a Japanese officer, Iwaichi Fujiwara, and led by an Indian officer captured in Malaya, Mohan Singh. It recruited Indian POWs held in Singapore camps. Its methods were observed by Muhammad Ismail Khan, the Baluch Regiment officer who had captured a Japanese soldier at Kota Bharu in December 1941. He later recalled a propaganda speech given by Mohan Singh in his camp:

> [He] said that we must join the Japanese, we must join the Indian National Army under his command and then fight for the freedom of India. The British have got no strength left to fight. They're in full flight in Burma and the Japanese will soon be in India.

Sikh traitor
Ronald Searle
Singapore 1944

Khan resisted frequent INA attempts to gain his allegiance, which included the threat that 'we would all be shot if we don't join'. Some 20,000 Indian POWs did sign up for the INA at this time, rising later to over 40,000. From June 1943, the INA was commanded by Subhas Chandra Bose, a former President of the Indian National Congress whose adventurous wartime experiences had included time spent in Hitler's Germany where he created the Indian Legion – a precursor of the INA recruited from Indian POWs captured in North Africa. Bose wanted the INA to play a leading role in the Japanese invasion of India and the fomenting of a general uprising against the British. This was not to Tokyo's liking and only a much-reduced INA contingent was permitted to participate in the 1944 Imphal offensive. Although INA troops saw action elsewhere too, their impact was modest and far below that dreamed of by Bose. Tokyo granted him a political reward of sorts by allowing him to proclaim the Provisional Government of Free India (Azad Hind) in October 1943, based first in Singapore and later in Rangoon. As a further token of Japanese goodwill, Bose's government was given a measure of administrative control in the Andaman and Nicobar Islands, thus conferring upon it a kind of territorial legitimacy. Bose was killed in an aircraft accident in August 1945, but his charisma, nationalist fervour and considerable popular appeal long outlived him. This, and heavy-handed British prosecution of INA personnel after the war, fed significantly into events leading to India's independence, and partition, in 1947.

A major Allied casualty of the immediate post-war years was Chiang Kai-shek. A flawed leader of men, on the international stage he often bathed in the reflected glory of his formidable wife, Madam Chiang. During the war the Generalissimo was considerably less interested in fighting the Japanese than in defeating his domestic communist enemies, but Chiang and his increasingly corrupt KMT regime were no match for their single-minded and fanatical leader Mao Zedong. It was Mao's armed forces who had in most practical respects carried the main burden of China's war against Japan, and it was eventually Mao who prevailed in the country's protracted civil war. Chiang and the KMT leadership were forced to flee to Taiwan in 1949 when the People's Republic

Sketch of a Pro-Japanese Sikh Guard, Changi Gaol, 1944 by Ronald Searle. The artist wrote 'Sikh traitor' above the portrait but reasons for joining the Indian National Army were varied, ranging from idealism to coercion. Many INA personnel became POW camp guards, particularly in Singapore.

of China was proclaimed. Communist forces were also in the ascendant in French Indochina. During the war the Viet Minh guerrilla organisation under the ideological direction of Ho Chi Minh and the military leadership of Võ Nguyên Giáp fought both the Japanese and the French administration retained by them. A key factor in their success was substantial US backing, including assistance on the ground by Office of Strategic Services (OSS) agents. By the end of the war, the communists controlled most of northern Indochina and in September 1945 proclaimed the Democratic Republic of Vietnam. French attempts to re-establish colonial rule were only temporarily successful. Their fight against Giáp's soldiers ended in defeat at Dien Bien Phu in 1954, leading into the defining conflict of the post-1945 era, the Vietnam War.

Having contributed indirectly but significantly to the end of Western colonial rule in South-East Asia, Japan's own pre-war colonial story came to an end in September 1945. Marshal Vasilevsky's Soviet forces, after defeating the Japanese in Manchuria, advanced into northern Korea. In agreement with the Americans, they halted and occupied the country north of the 38th Parallel, while US forces occupied the south. The scene was thereby set for the Korean War of 1950–1953, the first major 'hot' conflict of what came to be called the Cold War. The war against Japan was receding into history, but it continued to cast a long shadow into the brave new world emerging from the profound upheaval of the Second World War.

A lighter moment between Mahatma Gandhi and Sir Stafford Cripps during the latter's 1942 mission to India. Gandhi dismissed the British government's offer of post-war Dominion status as a 'post-dated cheque drawn on a failing bank'.

MAPS

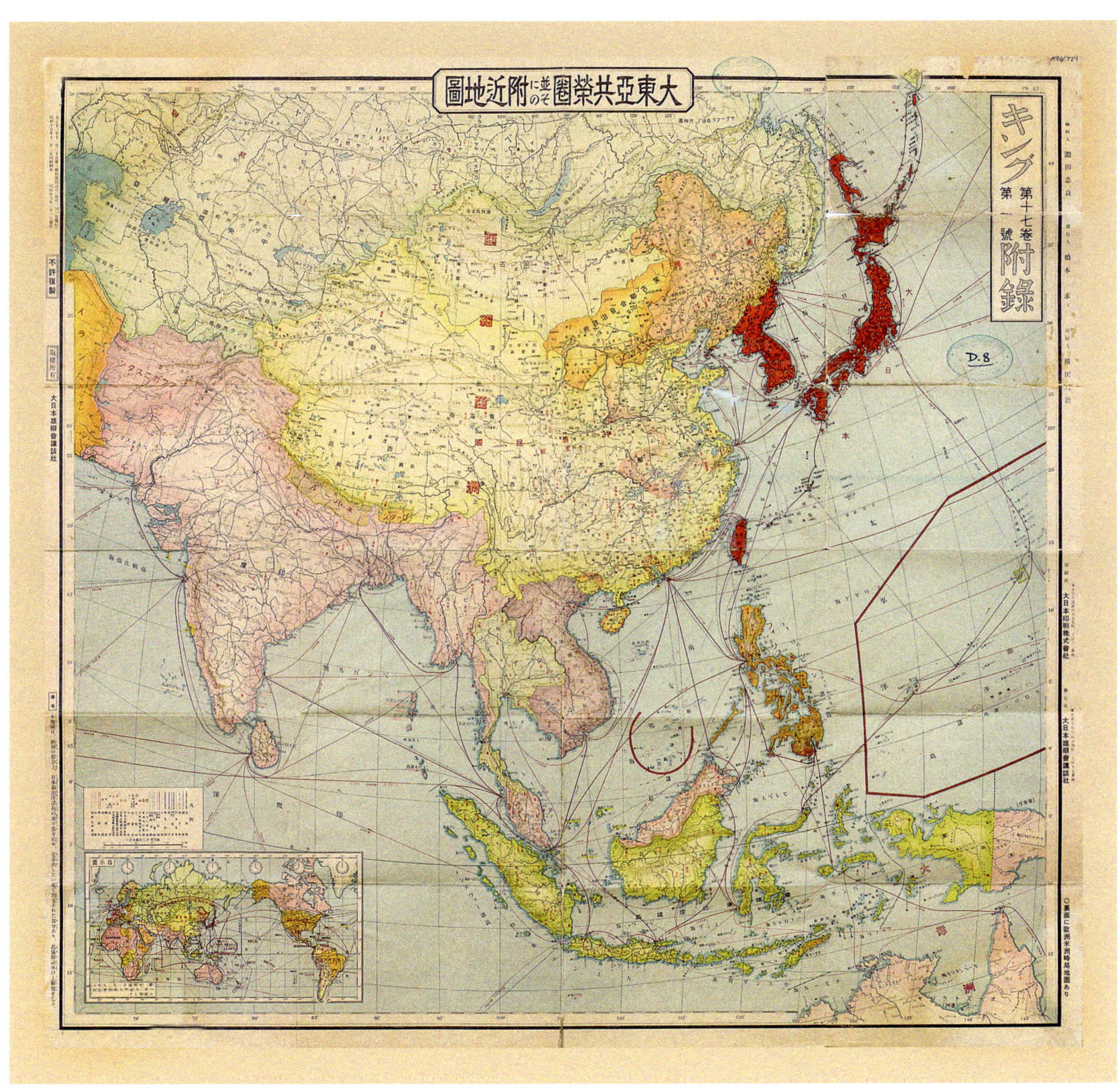

Japanese map of South-East Asia and the West Pacific Ocean, showing the Japanese occupation of Korea, Taiwan and half of Sakhalin Island.

Imphal & Kohima: Before the Monsoon breaks in Burma. ABCA Map Review 37, 27 March – 10 April 1944. The British fought a fierce defensive battle against the Japanese at Imphal and Kohima in Assam, near the Burma–India frontier, between March and June 1944.

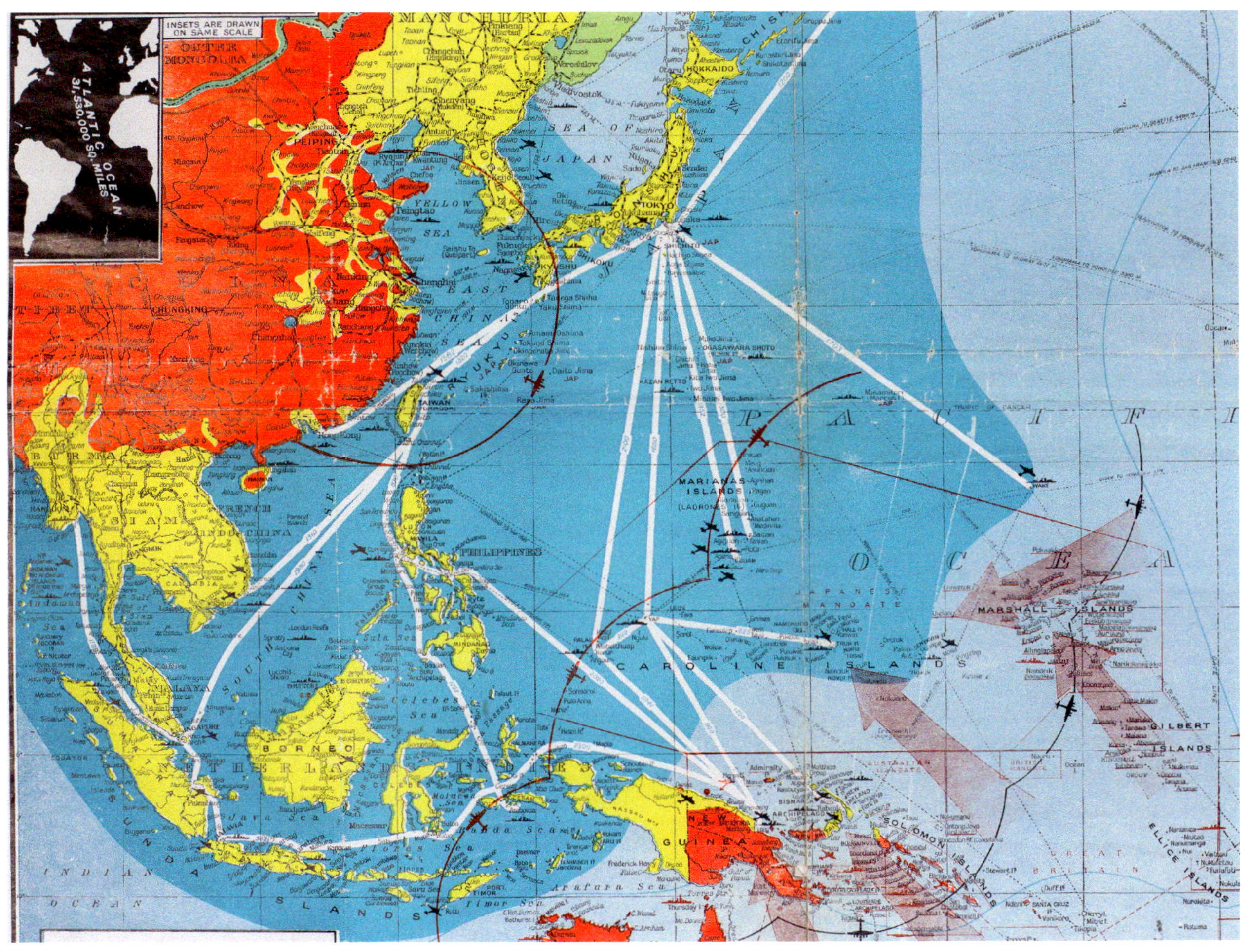

West Pacific, May 1944. Allied thrusts in red. After the Battle of Midway in 1942, the Americans launched their 'offensive-defensive' Pacific strategy, with axes of advance westward across the south and central Pacific.

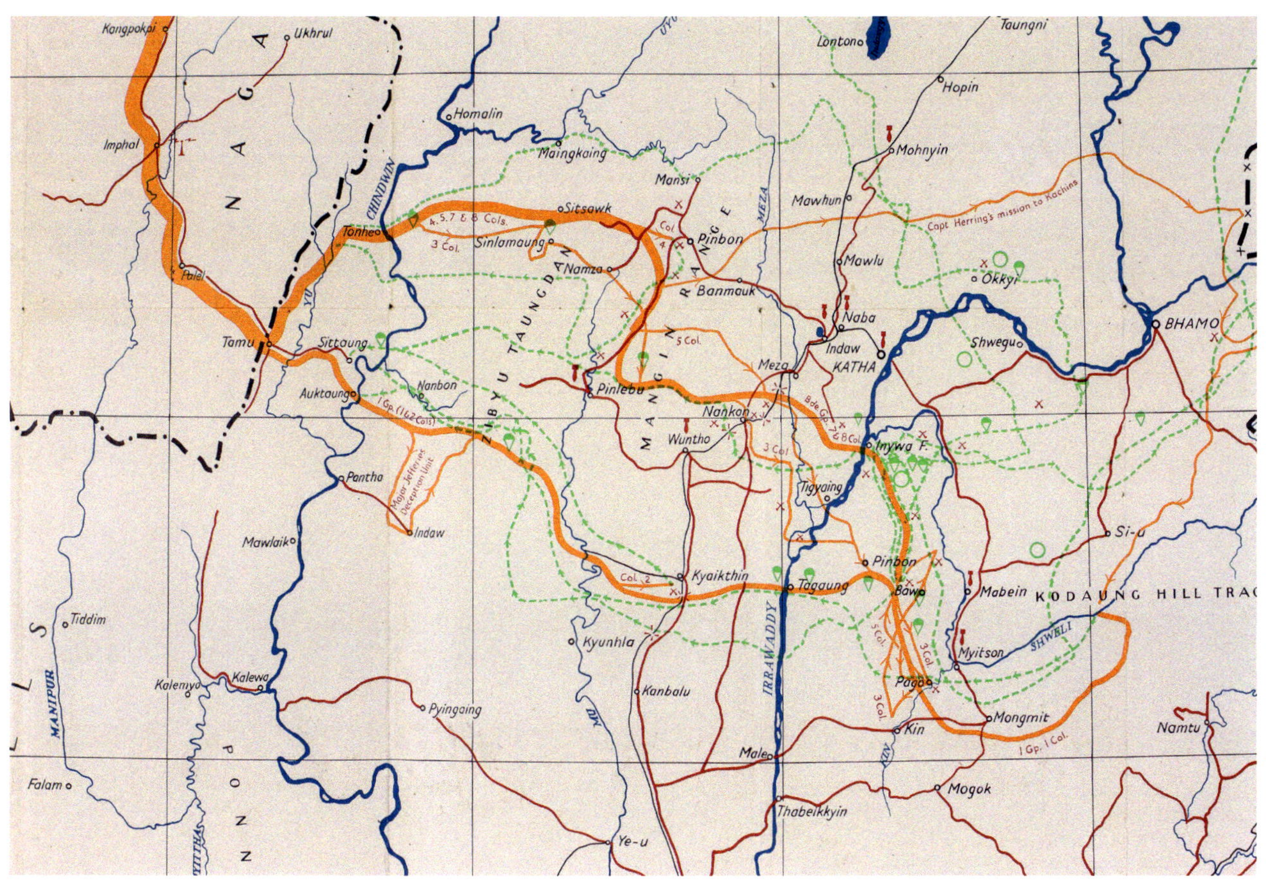

Chindits. *Operations in North Burma February–June 1943.* 77 Indian Infantry Brigade. Chindits were British columns (including Indian, Gurkha and African troops) conducting guerrilla warfare in the jungle against Japanese communications. The orange lines are column routes into Burma and the green ones are dispersal routes out. Parachutes indicate supply drops and the crossed swords show engagements.

Sources

IWM Documents © IWM unless otherwise stated

Private Papers of Allan Gerard OBE (Documents.27798) © Gillian Seymour

Private Papers of J E G (Jack) Egan (Documents.27742) © The Rights Holder

Private Papers of Arthur Sleep (Documents.25926) © The Estate of Arthur Sleep

Private Papers of Colonel C H D (Cyril) Wild MBE (Documents.18752)

Private Papers of Flight Lieutenant D S (Donald) Hill MBE (Documents.27698) © The Family of Donald Hill

Private Papers of L C (Lesley) Millington (Documents.20782) © The Millington Family

Through Japanese Eyes (Documents.8968) © Crown copyright reproduced under delegated authority from The Keeper of Public Records. Image: IWM (Documents.8968)

Private Papers of Captain A A (Andrew Atholl) Duncan (Documents.22834) © The Rights Holder

Private Papers of Lily Judah (Documents.27934) © The Rights Holder

Private Papers of Miss M (Margaret) Dryburgh (Documents.4395) © The Rights Holder

Private Papers of Peter Booth (Documents.27258) © The Rights Holder

Private Papers of Father J Siemes (Documents.3146) © The Rights Holder

Private Papers of Mrs N (Noelle) Williams (Documents.949) © The Estate of Noelle Williams

IWM Sound Archive © IWM unless otherwise stated

Burton Stein (8640)

Muhammad Ismail Khan (11748)

Neville Graham Hogan (12342)

Robert Malcolm Morris (20468)

James Michael Calvert (9942)

Charles Alfred William Aves (15486)

Benjamin Thomas Cattle (20363)

Reginald Amos Bandy (21051)

Other

Toland, John, *The Rising Sun* (London: Pen and Sword, 2016)

Carver, Michael, *The War Lords* (London: Pen and Sword, 1976)

FDR's Papers as President – Master Speech File 1401: Fireside Chat #18 regarding War with Japan, December 9, 1941, courtesy of the National Archives and Records Association

Swinson, Arthur, *Four Samurai* (London: Hutchinson, 1968)

Charter of the United Nations and Statute of the International Court of Justice (1945) © United Nations

Images

All images are IWM © unless otherwise stated

Introduction

EN 10898, Art.IWM PST 16863, © Alex Gordon (Art.IWM ART 16712 1)

Chapter One

A 4821, WEA 4018, FLA 205, HU 48784, HU 55635, HU 53134, HU 36523, NYP 22544

Chapter Two

HU 2785, EN 21474, HU 36485, NYP 68079, Art.IWM PST 5818, OEM 21469, MH 5952, Courtesy USA Government (Documents.11712)

Chapter Three

HU 2776, KF 89, MH 33566, K 1228, © The Rights Holder (HU 2675), FE 49, A 9692, KF 102, K 702, MH 30186, HU 3378, © Ronald Searle (Art.IWM ART 15747 3), HU 2781, FLA 2449, © Grandaughter of Charles Thrale (Art.IWM ART 15417 1)

Chapter Four

KF 112, KF 189, Art.IWM ART LD 5830, KF 114, HU 2780, HU 2766, HU 2779

Chapter Five

CI 1283, COL 223, IND 2917, SE 2138, IB 283, INS 5272, EPH 1855, HU 70592, K 9316, IND 7049, Documents.0960, HU 70508, IND 3714, Art.IWM ART LD 5687, EPH 9909

Chapter Six

AUS 2037, EN 33586, NYP 60749, INS 4653, NYP 52815, NY 6397, NYF 42432, FLA 5501, K 5866

Chapter Seven

Art.IWM ART LD 5618, MH 28352, © Ronald Searle (Art.IWM ART 15747 42), HU 92336, EPH 581, © Alex Gordon (Art.IWM ART 16712 1), EPH 685, EPH 10026, EPH 800, COM 567, EPH 9321, HU 43990, Art.IWM ART LD 5620, EPH 9973, EPH 8514

Chapter Eight

NYF 74928, Art.IWM PST 0177, EPH 1030, A 25544, NYF 30343, Art.IWM ART 15452, HU 51237, EPH 11740, A 30555, IND 4740, HU 44878, MH 29447, FRE 11910, MH 2629, LBY E. 88 / 165, HU 57914

Chapter Nine

A 30426, IND 4845, FLA 5503, Art.IWM ART LD 5824, A 30522, NAP 281858, SE 4450

Chapter Ten

SE 5652, © The Rights Holder (Art.IWM PST 9449), INS 893, © Ronald Searle (Art.IWM ART 15747 145 a), IND 740

Maps

M90 / 729, 4029, MD 12255, MD 14822

About the Author

Stephen Walton is a Senior Curator in the Second World War & Mid-20th Century Conflict team and is based at IWM Duxford. He joined IWM in 1990 as an Archivist, working on the museum's extensive collections of letters, diaries, unpublished memoirs and other documents of service personnel and civilians during both World Wars. He is the author of *The D-Day Landings* in the IWM Photography Collection series and has written the introductions to a number of titles in the IWM Wartime Classics series.

Acknowledgements

The author would like to thank the IWM Publishing team for making this book possible, in particular Madeleine James, Lara Bateman and Sarah Newman. Invaluable advice and guidance was also provided by IWM colleagues James Taylor, Ian Kikuchi, Adrian Kerrison and Christian Wellard (now at the Royal Armouries). Anthony Richards facilitated access to newly-transcribed oral history material in the museum's Sound collections. The author also owes a debt of gratitude to the donors and holders of copyright in the various Documents collections quoted from in this book, particular and personal thanks go to Meg Parkes (daughter of Andrew Duncan) and Christopher Hill (son of Donald Hill), also to Violet Musry and Tamara Brecher for sharing Lily Judah's story.

Index

Page numbers in italics refer to illustration captions.

C